Introdu

Welcome to "Self-Care Ways to Prioritize Your Well-Being"! I'm thrilled to embark on this journey with you, exploring the wonderful world of self-care without breaking the bank.

In a world that often bombards us with images of luxurious spa retreats and high-end wellness products, it's easy to fall into the trap of thinking that self-care comes with a hefty price tag. But fear not! This book is here to debunk that myth and show you that prioritizing your well-being can be both accessible and budget-friendly.

We all know that taking care of ourselves is essential, but sometimes our wallets don't seem to agree. Whether you're a college student on a tight budget, a young professional starting out, or anyone who wants to make self-care a daily practice without draining your bank account, this book is designed with you in mind.

Together, we'll explore practical strategies, creative solutions, and simple yet effective tips to make self-care a natural part of your routine, no matter what your financial situation looks like. After all, self-care isn't a luxury; it's a necessity for a healthy and fulfilling life.

So, grab a cozy blanket, find your favorite reading spot, and let's embark on a journey to discover the joy of self-care on a budget. Because taking care of yourself shouldn't cost a fortune, and your well-being deserves to be a top priority. Let's dive in!

Definition of Self-Care

Alright, let's kick things off by getting on the same page about what we mean when we talk about self-care. It's not just a buzzword or an excuse for a spa day (although, don't get me wrong, spa days are fantastic!). Self-care is all about intentionally doing things that promote our physical, mental, and emotional well-being.

Think of it as giving yourself the same TLC (tender loving care) that you readily offer to your friends, family, or even that potted plant on your windowsill. It's about recognizing your own needs and taking actions that nurture and replenish your mind, body, and spirit.

Self-care isn't a one-size-fits-all kind of deal. It's a personal journey, and what works for one person might not work for another. Whether it's taking a quiet moment with a cup of tea, going for a walk, or simply enjoying a good book, self-care is about finding what makes you feel good and incorporating it into your routine.

So, as we dive into the world of self-care on a budget, remember this: it's not about fancy gadgets or spending big bucks. It's about discovering the small, meaningful ways you can show yourself some love without emptying your wallet. Get ready to redefine self-care, my friend!

Importance of Prioritizing Well-Being

Now that we've nailed down what self-care is all about, let's talk about why it's crucial to put your well-being at the top of your to-do list. Picture this: life is like a non-stop rollercoaster, and you're strapped in for the ride. There are highs, lows, unexpected loops, and the occasional upside-down twist.

In the midst of this whirlwind, it's easy to forget about the person riding the rollercoaster – you! That's where self-care swoops in like a superhero cape. It's your secret weapon to help you not just survive but thrive on this rollercoaster adventure.

Taking care of yourself isn't selfish; it's a smart move. When you prioritize your well-being, you're better equipped to handle the twists and turns life throws at you. Imagine having a mental and emotional toolkit ready to tackle challenges head-on. That's what self-care does – it gives you the tools to face whatever comes your way with resilience and a smile.

So, as we delve into affordable ways to make self-care a daily habit, remember this: you're not just pampering yourself; you're investing in the superhero version of you. Get ready to explore practical strategies that not only fit your budget but also empower you to take charge of your well-being. It's time to make self-care a priority, and you're the star of this show!

Acknowledging Financial Constraints

Hey there! Now that we're all gung-ho about self-care and ready to prioritize our well-being, let's have an honest chat about the F-word – finances. Yep, money. We get it – budgets can be tight, and the thought of adding another expense to the mix might feel like trying to fit a giraffe into a Mini Cooper. Tricky, right?

But fear not! We're in this together, and this chapter is all about acknowledging those financial constraints and finding ways to sprinkle a little self-care magic into your life without making your wallet run for the hills.

Think of it like this: just because your bank account isn't doing the cha-cha doesn't mean you can't treat yourself to some well-deserved TLC. We're about to discover budget-friendly self-care that'll leave you feeling like a million bucks without spending anywhere close to that.

So, grab your financial superhero cape (if you don't have one, metaphorical capes totally count!), and let's navigate the world of self-care on a budget like the savvy money-saving champions we are. Ready? Let's dive in!

Making Self-Care Accessible on a Budget

Alright, buckle up for the exciting part! We've covered what self-care is, why it's like adding rocket fuel to your well-being, and even given a friendly nod to your financial situation. Now, let's talk about why you cracked open this book in the first place.

The mission? Making self-care your BFF without sending your piggy bank into therapy. This book is your guide, your trusty sidekick, in navigating the world of affordable self-care. We're about to unravel a treasure trove of tips, tricks, and hacks that won't drain your wallet but will fill up your self-care cup (we promise, it's a big cup).

So, if you've ever felt like your well-being was doing a disappearing act because of budget concerns, worry no more. We're here to show you that you can be the captain of your self-care ship, steering through calm waters even when the financial seas get a bit choppy.

Ready to explore budget-friendly self-care ideas that'll make you feel like you just won the lottery of life? Let's dive into the adventure and make self-care not just a buzzword but a practical, doable, and delightful part of your everyday routine. Ready, set, self-care on a budget – let's go! 🚀✨

Chapter 1: Understanding Self-Care on a Budget

Hey there, Self-Care Trailblazers! Welcome to the first pit stop on our journey to a well-nourished, happy you. In this chapter, we're going to dive deep into the concept of self-care on a budget. Get ready to toss aside any notions that self-care is only for the elite spa-goers or trust-fund babies because, guess what? It's for you, me, and everyone in between!

We'll unravel the mystery behind budget-friendly self-care, dispelling myths and misconceptions like the magical wizards we are. So, grab your metaphorical magnifying glass (real ones work too) and let's explore the wonderful world of self-care that won't make your wallet shed a tear. Ready for some budget-friendly self-love? Let's get into it! 🫶💥

Debunking Self-Care Myths

Alright, my fellow self-care enthusiasts, let's kick off this journey by dismantling a few myths that might be lingering in the air like pesky mosquitoes. Grab your myth-busting hat (yes, it's a thing now) because we're diving headfirst into the magical realm of self-care on a budget!

Myth #1: Self-Care is Just for the Rich and Famous

Let's address the elephant in the room – the misconception that self-care is only for those living in a mansion with a golden bathtub and a personal masseuse on standby. Newsflash: self-care is not reserved for the elite. It's not about the price tag on your face mask or the cost of your yoga mat. It's about intentional, mindful practices that rejuvenate your mind, body, and spirit. So, wave goodbye to the idea that you need a trust fund to indulge in self-care; we're here to make it accessible for all.

Myth #2: Self-Care Requires Lavish Spa Days

Picture this: a day at an opulent spa, surrounded by scented candles, soothing music, and fluffy robes. While that sounds divine, it's not the only route to self-care nirvana. Sure, spa days are fantastic, but they're not the be-all and end-all of self-care. We're about to explore a universe of budget-friendly self-care options that don't involve maxing out your credit card. From DIY spa days at home to simple mindfulness exercises, we've got a variety of tools in our self-care toolbox.

Myth #3: Self-Care is Time-Consuming

Raise your hand if you've ever thought, "I'd love to practice self-care, but who has the time?" Well, put that hand down and shake off the time myth. Self-care doesn't have to be a lengthy affair. In fact, some of the most powerful self-care practices can be woven seamlessly into your daily routine. We're talking about quick, effective rituals that won't have you setting your alarm an hour earlier or sacrificing your lunch break. Because, let's face it, ain't nobody got time for that!

Myth #4: Self-Care is All About Material Things

Yes, that fancy lavender-scented candle can set the mood, but self-care isn't confined to the material realm. It's about nurturing your soul, not just your surroundings. While we'll explore some tangible tools for self-care, we'll also dive into the intangible – practices that cost nothing but can yield priceless results. From gratitude journaling to mindful breathing, get ready to embrace the non-material side of self-care.

Now that we've tossed these myths out the window like confetti, you might be wondering, "What exactly is self-care, then?" Great question! Let's dive into the heart of it in the next section.

Defining Self-Care in the Real World

So, we've established that self-care isn't an exclusive club for the wealthy, spa enthusiasts, or time-rich individuals. But what is it really, especially in the context of our everyday lives? Let's break it down.

At its core, self-care is the intentional act of taking care of your own well-being. It's about recognizing your own needs and taking steps to meet them, just like you would for a friend. It's not a one-size-fits-all situation; it's as unique as you are.

Self-care encompasses a broad spectrum of activities, ranging from the simple and mundane to the indulgent and luxurious. It's about finding what resonates with you, what makes you feel alive, refreshed, and balanced.

For some, self-care might involve a morning meditation, a brisk walk in the park, or savoring a cup of tea in blissful solitude. For others, it could mean dancing like nobody's watching, losing themselves in a good book, or practicing gratitude before bedtime. The key is to identify what brings you joy, peace, and a sense of connection to yourself.

In the upcoming chapters, we'll explore these varied facets of self-care, tailoring them to fit snugly into the nooks and crannies of your budget and daily routine. So, get ready to redefine self-care in your terms, banish the myths, and embrace the adventure ahead. Self-care on a budget is not just a possibility; it's your new reality. Let's dive in, my fellow myth-busters! 🚀✨

The Priceless Essence of Budget-Friendly Self-Care

Now that we've thrown the myths out the window like confetti, it's time to uncover the true essence of self-care on a budget. We're not just talking about cutting costs; we're talking about enriching your life without breaking the bank. So, grab your metaphorical magnifying glass, Sherlock, because we're about to explore the priceless world of budget-friendly self-care.

The Budget-Friendly Mindset

First things first – let's shift our mindset. Budget-friendly self-care isn't about settling for less; it's about being savvy, creative, and intentional. It's like upgrading from a regular latte to a frothy cappuccino without the extra cost – the essence remains, but the approach is a bit more resourceful.

Think of it as a dance with your budget, a tango where you lead and your financial situation gracefully follows. We're not looking to tighten belts here; we're aiming for a harmonious balance that lets you indulge in self-care without sending your budget into a tailspin.

Identifying Affordable Luxuries

In the realm of budget-friendly self-care, we're all about discovering affordable luxuries – those little joys that add a touch of magic to your day. Maybe it's a moment of stillness in the morning, a warm shower after a long day, or the simple pleasure of curling up with a good book. These luxuries don't come with a hefty price tag, but their impact is immeasurable.

Think about it. When was the last time you treated yourself to something that didn't cost a fortune? That's the sweet spot we're aiming for – the delightful intersection of accessible and indulgent. It's about finding the luxurious in the everyday, the extraordinary in the ordinary.

Budgeting for Well-Being

Now, let's chat about everyone's favorite topic – budgets. I know, the mere mention of the word might send shivers down your spine, but fear not. Budgeting for well-being is not about complicated spreadsheets or financial acrobatics. It's about aligning your spending with your priorities, with a special emphasis on the priority that is you.

Take a moment to assess your budget. What are the non-negotiables? Rent or mortgage, utilities, groceries – these are the essentials. But guess what? Your well-being is also non-negotiable. Allocating a portion of your budget to self-care isn't an extravagance; it's an investment in your mental, emotional, and physical health.

Consider it a well-being fund, a dedicated space in your budget where self-care takes center stage. It doesn't have to be a grand production; even a modest allocation can work wonders. Whether it's a monthly book splurge, a cozy blanket fund, or a reserve for a weekend adventure, earmarking funds for self-care transforms it from an afterthought to a priority.

Setting Realistic Financial Goals

Now, let's talk goals – not the climb-Mount-Everest kind (unless that's your thing), but the achievable, realistic goals that make budget-friendly self-care a sustainable practice.

Start small. Maybe your goal is to treat yourself to a coffee from your favorite cafe once a week or set aside a few dollars each month for a self-care splurge. The key is to make these goals realistic and tailored to your financial landscape. This isn't about keeping up with the Kardashians; it's about keeping up with your own well-being in a way that feels good for you and your wallet.

In the upcoming chapters, we'll delve into the practical side of budget-friendly self-care, exploring everyday practices, outdoor adventures, nourishing your body, and more. Get ready to discover the joy of indulging in affordable luxuries, dancing with your budget, and setting financial goals that prioritize your well-being. The adventure has just begun, and the best part? The budget-friendly magic is about to unfold. Are you ready to make self-care an essential and affordable part of your life? Let's continue this journey together! 🎇 🎆

Embracing Financial Realities with a Smile

Hey there, Budget Buddies! Now that we've got our mindset and budgeting capes on, let's tackle the sometimes intimidating topic of acknowledging our financial constraints with a friendly grin. Yes, you read that right – we're going to make friends with our wallets and dance through the budgetary maze with a smile.

The Budget-Friendly Grin

First things first, let's face it – we're not all swimming in pools of gold coins like Scrooge McDuck. We get it; life throws curveballs, and wallets sometimes sound like they're sighing with relief when we're not looking. But fear not, because the key here is to embrace our financial reality with a sense of humor and a sprinkle of optimism.

Picture this: you open your wallet, and it gives you a wink instead of a frown. That's the budget-friendly grin we're aiming for. It's the acknowledgment that, yes, we might not have unlimited funds, but we do have the power to make the most of what we've got. So, let's turn our financial frowns upside down and dive into the joyous world of self-care on a budget.

Being Kind to Your Wallet

Now, being kind to your wallet doesn't mean neglecting your needs. It means treating your finances with the same compassion you'd extend to a friend who's had a rough day. It's about finding ways to pamper yourself without causing financial stress.

We're going to become financial ninjas, my friends – stealthily navigating the world of budget-friendly self-care and leaving our wallets intact. Whether your wallet is on a diet or just watching its steps, we're here to make the journey enjoyable, not a burden.

Affordable Self-Care: It's a Thing

Let's bust another myth while we're at it – the idea that self-care has to come with a hefty price tag. Not true! In fact, some of the most effective and fulfilling self-care practices don't cost a dime. From a calming deep breath to a heartfelt laugh with friends, the currency here is intention, not dollars.

We're going to explore affordable self-care practices that will make your wallet do a little happy dance. Think of it as finding treasures in the budget-friendly jungle of well-being. Spoiler alert: these treasures might not be gold doubloons, but they're priceless in terms of how they make you feel.

Balancing Act: Wants vs. Needs

Now, let's talk about balance – the delicate seesaw between wants and needs. Self-care is a need, no doubt about it. But in the land of budget-friendly self-care, we're also mindful of our wants. It's about finding that sweet spot where your well-being gets the attention it deserves without sending your budget into a tailspin.

Think of it as a delicious dish where the flavors of necessity and desire come together. We're creating a budget-friendly feast for your well-being, with each element thoughtfully chosen to satisfy both the must-haves and the nice-to-haves.

Small Shifts, Big Impact

Here's the secret sauce – small shifts can lead to big impacts. We're not talking about a financial revolution here; we're talking about gentle, sustainable changes that make self-care a seamless part of your budget.

Maybe it's the decision to brew your own coffee instead of the daily café splurge, allowing you to redirect those saved dollars into your well-being fund. Or perhaps it's the conscious choice to opt for a budget-friendly online yoga class instead of an expensive studio membership.

In the upcoming chapters, get ready to embark on a journey of small, budget-friendly changes that will transform the way you approach self-care. We're navigating the seas of financial realities with a grin, finding joy in the small victories, and making self-care an everyday celebration. The budget-friendly adventure continues – are you ready for the next chapter? 🌈🎁

Chapter 2: Assessing Your Personal Budget

Welcome to Chapter 2, where we're putting on our financial detective hats and diving into the heart of budget magic. Assessing your personal budget might sound about as thrilling as watching paint dry, but fear not! We're about to turn budgeting into a friendly, empowering adventure. Imagine it like a treasure map, and the treasure at the end? A well-nourished, happy you. So, grab your compass (or your favorite budgeting app) and get ready to explore the world of budget-friendly self-care. We're not looking to create budget masterpieces; we're aiming for something more practical – a budget that not only pays the bills but also sets aside a little treasure for your well-being. Together, we'll navigate the financial landscape, identify the nooks and crannies where self-care dollars hide, and make budgeting not just about numbers but about creating a life that feels good. Ready for this financial adventure? Let's set sail! 🗺️💰

Creating a Basic Budget Framework

Ahoy, budget explorers! Ready to embark on the first leg of our financial adventure? Today, we're going to create a basic budget framework that's as user-friendly as your favorite emoji. Think of it as crafting a roadmap to navigate the financial terrain – not with a compass and a quill, but with a spreadsheet and a smile.

Step 1: The Money In Dance

Let's start with the cha-cha of finance – the money in dance. This is where your income takes center stage, showcasing its fancy footwork. Write down your sources of income, whether it's your paycheck, side hustles, or that generous birthday check from Grandma. Think of it as a dance floor where every dollar has its own groove, and your job is to choreograph the financial dance of your life.

Step 2: The Money Out Waltz

Next up, we have the money out waltz – the elegant dance of expenses. This is where you list all your monthly expenses, from the necessities like rent, utilities, and groceries to the occasional date night or that subscription to your favorite cat meme service. Don't forget those sneaky, irregular expenses like birthday gifts or annual insurance premiums; they're part of the waltz too. It's a balancing act, ensuring that every dollar has its dance partner and none are left twiddling their thumbs on the sidelines.

Step 3: Finding Your Rhythm

Now that you've witnessed the financial dance-off, it's time to find your rhythm. Subtract your total expenses from your total income. If the number makes you want to do a victory dance, fantastic! You're in the positive territory. If it's more of a cha-cha-cha to break even, that's okay too. We're here to adjust the dance moves and make sure your financial steps are in harmony with your goals.

Step 4: Adjusting the Playlist

Think of your budget as a dynamic playlist, not a rigid setlist. Life's melodies change, and so should your budget. If the numbers aren't playing the tune you want, it's time to adjust the playlist. Can you cut back on the dining-out duets and add more strings to your savings symphony? Maybe the streaming services quartet needs a reshuffle. Be the DJ of your budget, creating a playlist that not only meets your financial needs but also leaves room for the songs of well-being.

Step 5: The Emergency Encore

Life is full of surprise encores – the car breaking down, the surprise medical bill, or the spontaneous road trip with friends. That's where the emergency fund takes the stage. Set aside a portion of your budget for this unsung hero. It's like having a financial umbrella for the unexpected rain showers. Trust me, future you will thank present you for this thoughtful budgetary inclusion.

Step 6: Celebrate the Victories

Every budgeting milestone deserves a celebration, whether it's paying off a credit card, reaching a savings goal, or successfully sticking to your budget for a month. Treat yourself to a budget-friendly victory dance – maybe a homemade dessert, a cozy movie night, or a solo dance party in your living room. Celebrating the wins, big or small, keeps the financial dance floor vibrant and encourages you to keep refining your moves.

Creating a basic budget framework is like choreographing the financial ballet of your life. It's not about strict rules and rigid routines; it's about finding a rhythm that lets you dance through life with confidence and joy. So, my fellow budget ballerinas and financial foxtrotters, let's continue this dance with our wallets and create a budget that's as flexible as it is friendly. The adventure has just begun! 🩰🎶

Identifying Discretionary Spending

Hello budget buddies, ready for the next groove in our financial dance? Today, we're putting on our detective hats and diving into the world of discretionary spending. Think of it as uncovering the secret agents in your budget, the spending categories that have a bit more flexibility, allowing you to make intentional choices that align with your financial goals. So, grab your magnifying glass, and let's embark on this budget detective mission with a friendly twist.

The Discretionary Detectives

First things first, let's meet our budget detectives. Discretionary spending includes those non-essential expenses that, while enjoyable, aren't absolute must-haves for survival. We're talking about dining out, entertainment, shopping sprees, and that extra shot of caramel in your morning coffee. These are the expenses that have a bit of wiggle room, making them prime candidates for optimization in our budget ballet.

The Budget Detective Toolkit

Now, how do we identify these undercover agents? It's time to unpack our budget detective toolkit:

1. Transaction Statements: Take a close look at your bank and credit card statements. What recurring charges and one-time splurges catch your eye? Identify those discretionary spending entries that might be camouflaged among the everyday necessities.

2. Your Favorite Budgeting App: If you're a fan of budgeting apps (they're like the sidekick in our

detective story), utilize categories to sort your spending. Highlight those categories that fall under the discretionary umbrella. Apps often do the heavy lifting, making it easier for you to spot the culprits.

3. Historical Spending Patterns: Reflect on your past spending habits. Are there months where your entertainment expenses skyrocketed or where you treated yourself a little too generously in the shopping department? Understanding your historical patterns provides valuable insights into areas where you can make strategic adjustments.

The Discretionary Decision Dance

Now that we've unmasked the discretionary spenders, it's time for the decision dance. Remember, discretionary spending isn't the villain; it's an opportunity for intentional choices. Here's how to twirl through this dance:

1. Prioritize Your Favorites: Identify the discretionary categories that bring you the most joy and align with your values. Love your weekly coffee shop visit? That's a keeper. Not as attached to your magazine subscription? It might be up for negotiation.

2. Set Limits: Embrace the power of limits. Establish a monthly cap for discretionary categories, giving yourself the freedom to indulge within those boundaries. It's like having guardrails on your spending

highway, ensuring you stay on the road to financial success.

3. Optimize Your Spending: Look for ways to optimize your discretionary spending. Can you find budget-friendly alternatives for your favorite activities? Maybe it's exploring free community events, swapping the fancy gym for home workouts, or DIY-ing that spa day.

4. Embrace the Joy of Saving: Redirect a portion of your discretionary budget toward savings or debt repayment. It's like turning your spending into a superhero – not only does it bring you joy, but it also contributes to your financial goals.

The Budget Detective Victory Lap

As you navigate the world of discretionary spending, remember, it's not about deprivation; it's about conscious choices. By identifying and managing these discretionary areas, you're not only optimizing your budget but also aligning your spending with what truly matters to you.

So, fellow budget detectives, put on your dancing shoes, grab your discretionary magnifying glass, and let's twirl through the budget ballroom with intention and flair. The financial dance continues, and you're the star of the show! 🕵️‍♀️🕵️‍♂️♂️

Allocating Funds for Self-Care within Your Budget

Hey there, financial architects! Now that we've mastered the dance of income and expenses, it's time to carve out a special space in our budget for the true VIP – your well-being. Picture it as creating a cozy, well-decorated room within the mansion of your budget, dedicated to self-care. Ready to sprinkle a little self-care magic into your financial blueprint? Let's dive in with a friendly flair.

The Well-Being Nook

Imagine your budget as a house, and within that house, there's a nook – a special corner reserved just for you, your happiness, and your well-being. This nook is where self-care gets its own comfy chair and a soft blanket, ready for you to curl up and indulge in the joy of taking care of yourself.

Setting the Well-Being Budget

Now, how do we set up this well-being nook within our budget mansion? It's time for a bit of budget feng shui:

1. Define Your Self-Care Priorities: What brings you the most joy and relaxation? Whether it's a monthly massage, a cozy reading nook, or a regular yoga class,

identify the self-care activities that light up your well-being radar.

2. Assign Dollar Values: Once you've pinpointed your self-care priorities, assign dollar values to them. How much would you feel comfortable allocating to each activity? This step transforms your self-care wishlist into tangible budget numbers.

3. Integrate into Your Monthly Budget: Now comes the magic – integrate these self-care allocations into your monthly budget. Treat them as non-negotiable line items, just like your rent or groceries. This sends a powerful message to yourself that your well-being is a top financial priority.

Balancing Act: Wants vs. Needs

In the world of budgeting, there's a delicate balance between wants and needs. While self-care might fall under the "want" category, it's a want that aligns with a deeper need – the need for a balanced, joyful life. As you allocate funds for self-care, recognize that you're not indulging in frivolous spending; you're investing in your mental, emotional, and physical well-being.

The Well-Being Emergency Fund

Just as every house needs an emergency fund for unexpected repairs, your well-being nook deserves a cushion for those surprise self-care opportunities. Maybe your favorite yoga studio has a flash sale, or there's a last-minute opening at the spa. Having a little extra in your well-being emergency fund allows you to seize these opportunities without disrupting your budget ballet.

Celebrating Self-Care Wins

Allocating funds for self-care is a win in itself, but let's take it a step further – celebrate those self-care victories! Did you stick to your well-being budget for the month? Treat yourself to a little extra self-care, whether it's a homemade spa night or a leisurely afternoon with a good book. Celebrating your wins creates a positive feedback loop, reinforcing the importance of self-care in your financial journey.

Adjusting Along the Way

Life is dynamic, and so is your well-being. As seasons change, so might your self-care priorities. Be open to adjusting your well-being budget along the way. Maybe a new interest sparks joy, or you find a budget-friendly alternative to an existing activity. Your well-being budget is a flexible canvas, ready to adapt to the evolving masterpiece of your life.

As you allocate funds for self-care within your budget, remember, you're not just managing dollars; you're curating a life that reflects your values and prioritizes your happiness. Your well-being nook is a sanctuary within the financial mansion, a space where joy and financial responsibility coexist in harmony. So, my fellow architects, let's build this well-being haven and infuse our budget with the magic of self-care. The journey continues, and the well-being nook is just a budget line away! 🏠 ♡

Setting Realistic Financial Goals for Well-Being

Greetings, goal-setters! Now that we've furnished our budget with a well-being nook, let's sprinkle a bit of stardust on our financial journey by setting realistic financial goals for well-being. Think of it as creating a treasure map with well-being gems, guiding you towards a life that's not just financially sound but brimming with joy. So, grab your map and let's chart a course for well-being riches!

Understanding Well-Being Goals

Well-being goals are like the North Star of your financial universe – guiding you in the direction of a happier, healthier life. These goals go beyond the traditional financial milestones; they're the unique markers that make your heart skip a beat. Whether it's a monthly spa day, a weekend retreat, or investing in that art class you've been eyeing, well-being goals add a touch of magic to your financial journey.

Identifying Your Well-Being North Star

What makes your heart sing? Take a moment to identify your well-being North Star. Is it a daily meditation practice, a regular fitness routine, or the thrill of exploring new hobbies? Your well-being goals should align with your values, bringing a sense of fulfillment and joy to your everyday life.

Quantifying Well-Being: Dollars and Sense

Now comes the exciting part – quantifying well-being in dollars and sense. Assign a financial value to your well-being goals. How much do you need to allocate in your budget to make these goals a reality? Whether it's a specific monthly amount for a wellness subscription or a lump sum for an annual retreat, attaching a dollar value makes your well-being goals tangible and achievable.

Creating a Well-Being Goal Timeline

Every treasure map needs a timeline, and your well-being goals are no exception. Break down your well-being goals into short-term, medium-term, and long-term targets. Short-term goals could be monthly self-care treats, medium-term might involve attending a wellness retreat within the year, while long-term goals could encompass significant investments like a home gym or a dream vacation. This timeline adds structure to your well-being journey, making it feel less like a wish list and more like a roadmap to success.

The Art of Goal Flexibility

Life is an ever-changing canvas, and so are your well-being goals. Be open to adjusting your goals as circumstances shift. Maybe a new interest takes center stage, or unexpected financial challenges arise. Flexibility is the key to a sustainable well-being journey. It's not about perfection; it's about progress and adapting your goals to suit the current rhythm of your life.

Balancing Short-Term Joys and Long-Term Thrills

As you set well-being goals, strike a balance between short-term joys and long-term thrills. Short-term goals provide instant gratification and keep the momentum alive, while long-term goals contribute to the overarching narrative of your well-being journey. Maybe a weekly coffee treat brings immediate joy, while saving for an annual wellness retreat fuels your long-term sense of well-being.

Measuring Success Beyond Dollars

While dollars play a role in quantifying well-being goals, the true measure of success goes beyond the financial realm. Take note of the non-monetary rewards – the increased sense of calm, improved physical health, or the joy derived from pursuing activities you love. Celebrate these intangible victories; they are the real treasures on your well-being map.

Celebrating Milestones on the Well-Being Journey

Each step toward a well-being goal is a milestone worth celebrating. Did you consistently stick to your fitness routine for a month? Treat yourself to a congratulatory dance party. Achieved a savings goal for a wellness retreat? Plan a small celebration to acknowledge your hard work. Celebrating milestones infuses joy into the journey and reinforces the positive impact of well-being goals on your life.

So, my fellow well-being explorers, let's set sail with our well-being treasure map, navigating the seas of financial goals with excitement and purpose. Your well-being is the ultimate treasure, and each goal you set is a step closer to unlocking its full potential. The adventure continues, and your well-being goals are the compass guiding you toward a life filled with happiness and fulfillment. Let's embark on this journey with enthusiasm and curiosity! 🗺️ ✨

Chapter 3:
Everyday Practices for
Affordable Self-Care

Ahoy, champions of self-care! Welcome to Chapter 3, where we're diving into the treasure trove of everyday practices for affordable self-care. Picture this chapter as a vibrant garden, blooming with budget-friendly flowers of joy, relaxation, and well-being. We're about to uncover the magic that exists in the mundane, the simple rituals that transform your day without putting a dent in your wallet. So, grab your gardening gloves (metaphorical or real – your call) and join us as we cultivate a landscape of affordable self-care practices that fit seamlessly into your daily routine. From morning rituals to evening delights, we're here to infuse your life with accessible, everyday self-care magic. Let's embark on this journey of cultivating joy, one affordable practice at a time! 🏵️ 🌿

Mindful Breathing Exercises

Greetings, mindful breathers! In this section, we're taking a deep dive into the world of mindful breathing – a pocket-sized powerhouse of calm in the chaos of our daily lives. Imagine it as a reset button for your mind, body, and spirit, accessible anytime, anywhere, and completely free. So, let's put on our imaginary oxygen masks (real ones work too, in a pinch) and embark on this journey of mindful breathing exercises that will have you feeling centered, refreshed, and ready to face the world with a smile.

The Magic of Mindful Breathing

Before we jump into the how-to, let's explore the magic behind mindful breathing. It's not just about inhaling and exhaling; it's about cultivating awareness of each breath, creating a tranquil oasis in the midst of life's hustle. Mindful breathing taps into the power of the present moment, inviting you to step off the treadmill of worries and into the sanctuary of your breath.

The 4-7-8 Breath: A Calming Symphony

One of the stars in the constellation of mindful breathing is the 4-7-8 breath, a simple yet potent exercise that feels like a calming symphony for your nervous system. Here's how to conduct this tranquil orchestra:

Step 1: Find Your Happy Place: Sit comfortably or lie down, whatever floats your mindful boat. Place the tip of your tongue against the ridge of tissue just behind your upper front teeth – a nifty detail that adds a dash of science to the art of breathing.

Step 2: The Inhale (Count of 4): Inhale quietly through your nose to a mental count of 4. Feel the breath fill your lungs like a gentle wave, expanding your chest and belly without straining.

Step 3: The Hold (Count of 7): Hold your breath for a count of 7, allowing the oxygen to permeate your cells and do its soothing dance. This pause is where the magic happens – it's like a suspenseful pause in your favorite song.

Step 4: The Exhale (Count of 8): Exhale audibly and completely through your mouth to the count of 8, releasing any tension or worries along with the breath. Picture the stress evaporating into the air like a dissipating cloud.

Step 5: Rinse and Repeat: Now, repeat the cycle three more times, and voila – you've just composed a symphony of calm within minutes. The 4-7-8 breath is your go-to melody for stressful moments, anxious nights, or whenever you need a dose of serenity.

Box Breathing: Your Portable Stress-Buster

If the 4-7-8 breath is a calming symphony, box breathing is your portable stress-buster – ready to whisk you away to a tranquil island of relaxation. Here's how to build your stress-busting box:

Step 1: Inhale (Count of 4): Inhale quietly through your nose to the count of 4, filling your lungs with a sense of calm and presence.

Step 2: Hold (Count of 4): Hold your breath for a count of 4, embracing the stillness and allowing your body to absorb the soothing effects of the breath.

Step 3: Exhale (Count of 4): Exhale slowly and completely through your mouth for a count of 4, releasing any tension or stress along with the breath.

Step 4: Pause (Count of 4): Hold your breath in its exhaled state for another count of 4, enjoying the brief pause before the next inhalation.

Step 5: Rinse and Repeat: Repeat the box breathing cycle for several rounds, syncing your breath with the counts. It's like a portable stress-busting toolkit at your fingertips, ready to use whenever you need a moment of tranquility.

The Breath of Fire: Energize Your Day

For a burst of energy and vitality, say hello to the breath of fire – a dynamic and invigorating breath exercise that's like a shot of espresso for your respiratory system. Here's how to ignite your inner fire:

Step 1: Find Your Grounding: Sit comfortably with a straight spine and place your hands on your knees or thighs. This is your launching pad for the breath of fire.

Step 2: Rapid Exhalations: Inhale deeply through your nose, and then exhale quickly and forcefully through your nose. It's like blowing out a series of birthday candles in rapid succession.

Step 3: Rhythmic Pace: Keep the breaths rhythmic and continuous, almost like a pulsating bellows. The emphasis is on the exhalation, and the inhalation happens naturally as a reflex to the rapid exhalations.

Step 4: Energize Your Being: Continue this rhythmic breath for 30 seconds to a minute, gradually building up to longer durations as you become more comfortable with the pace. Feel the surge of energy and warmth spreading throughout your body, awakening your senses and revitalizing your day.

Incorporating Mindful Breathing into Your Daily Symphony

Now that you've added these mindful breathing exercises to your self-care toolkit, the next step is to weave them into your daily symphony. Here are a few tips to seamlessly integrate mindful breathing into your routine:

1. Morning Serenade: Kickstart your day with a few minutes of mindful breathing. Whether it's the 4-7-8 breath to set a calm tone or the breath of fire to invigorate your senses, these exercises can be your morning serenade, preparing you for the day ahead.

2. Office Oasis: Amidst the hustle and bustle of work, steal a moment for mindful breathing. The beauty of these exercises lies in their portability – you can practice them at your desk, in a meeting (discreetly, of course), or during a short break.

3. Evening Wind-Down: As the day winds down, let mindful breathing be your wind-down ritual. Whether you opt for the soothing 4-7-8 breath or the stress-busting box breathing, these exercises can signal to your body that it's time to relax and transition into a restful evening.

4. Pre-Sleep Lullaby: End your day with a pre-sleep lullaby of mindful breathing. The rhythmic nature of these exercises can help quiet the mind, making it easier to drift into a peaceful slumber. Try the 4-7-8 breath or a few rounds of box breathing as part of your bedtime routine.

Creating Your Breathful Sanctuary

Incorporating mindful breathing into your daily routine isn't just a practice; it's a journey toward creating a breathful sanctuary in the midst of life's demands. These exercises, whether practiced individually or as part of a daily repertoire, offer a refuge of calm and presence. So, my fellow breathers, let the mindful symphony begin! Inhale the joy, exhale the stress, and embrace the transformative power of your breath. The everyday self-care adventure continues, and your breath is the gentle guide leading the way. 📖 🐚

DIY Spa Day at Home

Welcome, spa enthusiasts, to the blissful realm of DIY spa days at home! In this section, we're transforming your humble abode into a haven of relaxation and rejuvenation without breaking the bank. So, slip into your coziest robe, cue up the spa music playlist, and let's embark on a DIY spa day adventure that will leave you feeling pampered, refreshed, and ready to conquer the world.

Setting the Spa Day Stage

First things first, let's set the stage for your at-home spa extravaganza. Think of your space as a blank canvas awaiting the strokes of tranquility. Dim the lights, light some candles or fairy lights for that enchanting glow, and put on your favorite soothing tunes. The goal is to create an ambiance that transports you from the everyday hustle to a serene sanctuary.

DIY Face Mask Magic

No spa day is complete without a little face mask magic, and the best part is you can whip up effective masks using kitchen staples. For a hydrating boost, try a honey and avocado mask. Mash up a ripe avocado, mix it with a tablespoon of honey, and apply the luscious concoction to your face. Avocado nourishes your skin with vitamins, while honey provides a natural humectant, leaving your skin feeling supple and refreshed.

Epsom Salt Soak for Serenity

Turn your bath into a sanctuary with a simple yet luxurious Epsom salt soak. Epsom salt is a budget-friendly superstar that can help soothe sore muscles and promote relaxation. Add a cup or two of Epsom salt to your warm bath, toss in a few drops of your favorite essential oil (lavender is a classic choice), and let the stress melt away. Bonus points if you play some soft music or bring a good book to the tub!

Cucumber Eye Pads: Cool and Refreshing

Treat your eyes to a spa-worthy experience with DIY cucumber eye pads. Slice a cucumber into thin rounds, pop them in the fridge to chill, and place them over your closed eyes while you relax. The coolness of the cucumber reduces puffiness, and the refreshing sensation adds a touch of spa elegance to your DIY pampering session.

Coconut Oil Scalp Massage

Give your hair some love with a coconut oil scalp massage. Coconut oil is a multitasking marvel that nourishes your scalp and hair. Warm up a small amount of coconut oil (not too hot!), massage it into your scalp in gentle, circular motions, and let it work its magic for at least 30 minutes. Bonus points for wrapping your hair in a warm towel for an extra dose of relaxation. When you rinse, your hair will thank you with newfound softness and shine.

DIY Aromatherapy: The Power of Scents

Aromatherapy adds a layer of sensory delight to your DIY spa day. Create your own aromatherapy haven by using essential oils. Whether you prefer the calming scent of lavender, the uplifting aroma of citrus, or the grounding notes of eucalyptus, a few drops in a diffuser or even a bowl of hot water can turn your space into a fragrant oasis. Breathe in, and let the soothing scents transport you to a place of tranquility.

Tea Time for Inner Calm

No spa day is complete without a moment of reflection, and what better companion than a cup of herbal tea? Brew a cup of your favorite calming tea, whether it's chamomile, peppermint, or a soothing blend. Sip slowly, savoring each moment, and let the warmth of the tea infuse your DIY spa day with inner calm. Consider adding a touch of honey for a sweet treat that doubles as a natural humectant for your skin.

The Finishing Touch: Mindful Moments

As your DIY spa day draws to a close, take a few moments for mindfulness. Whether it's a short meditation, a gratitude journaling session, or simply basking in the post-spa glow, these mindful moments anchor the relaxation and extend the benefits of your at-home spa experience. It's the perfect way to transition back into the outside world with a sense of tranquility.

Affordable Luxury, Anytime You Need

The beauty of a DIY spa day at home is that it's not a one-time indulgence; it's an affordable luxury you can recreate whenever you need a little self-care boost. Whether you're unwinding after a hectic day, celebrating a personal milestone, or simply craving a dose of relaxation, your DIY spa day is ready to welcome you with open arms.

So, my fellow spa aficionados, let the DIY pampering begin! Transform your space into a sanctuary of serenity, indulge in the simple luxury of homemade masks and soaks, and let the tranquility of a spa day at home become a cherished part of your self-care routine. The adventure continues, and the spa awaits – enjoy every moment! 🛁 🪶

Incorporating Mindfulness into Daily Routines

Hey there, mindful mavens! In this section, we're diving into the art of weaving mindfulness into the fabric of your daily routines. Mindfulness isn't just reserved for meditation sessions on a mountaintop; it's a dynamic, accessible practice that can enhance every moment of your day. So, grab your metaphorical mindfulness cape (or an actual one if you have it), and let's explore how you can infuse your daily routines with the magic of mindfulness, creating a tapestry of presence, joy, and self-awareness.

Morning Mindful Moments

Let's kick off the day with a dose of morning mindfulness. Instead of jumping out of bed with your mind already racing through the day's to-do list, take a moment to savor the transition from sleep to wakefulness. Before reaching for your phone, spend a few minutes focusing on your breath. Notice the sensation of the air entering and leaving your body. Feel the warmth of the sunlight or the coziness of your blankets. This simple practice sets a mindful tone for the day, reminding you to embrace each moment with intention.

Mindful Mornings: Shower Edition

The morning shower – a daily ritual that often happens on autopilot. But what if you could turn this routine into a mindful oasis? As you feel the water cascading over you, bring your attention to the sensory experience. Notice the temperature of the water, the scent of your soap or shampoo, and the feeling of the water against your skin. Instead of mentally rehearsing the day ahead, let your mind bathe in the present moment. It's a simple shift that transforms a mundane task into a mini spa for your senses.

Mindful Bites: The Art of Eating

Elevate your meals from mere sustenance to a feast of mindfulness. Whether it's breakfast, lunch, or dinner, turn eating into a mindful practice. Engage your senses by appreciating the colors, textures, and aromas of your food. Take small, deliberate bites, savoring each flavor. Put down your phone, turn off the TV, and create a space for mindful eating. Not only does this enhance your appreciation for food, but it also fosters a healthier relationship with eating.

Workday Mindful Moments

Amidst the hustle of work, carve out mindful moments to pause and reset. Every hour, take a brief break to stretch, breathe, or simply gaze out the window. Instead of plowing through tasks with a sense of urgency, approach each one with focused attention. Whether you're responding to emails, attending meetings, or tackling projects, infuse a sprinkle of mindfulness into your work routine. It not only enhances your productivity but also brings a sense of calm to the busiest of days.

Commute Contemplation

If your daily routine involves a commute, turn it into a mindfulness opportunity. Whether you're driving, biking, or taking public transportation, resist the urge to view it as a chore. Instead, use this time for contemplation. Notice the scenery, feel the rhythm of your movements, and allow your mind to wander without the pressure of constant stimulation. It's a chance to transition between work and home with a mindful pause.

Evening Unwind: A Mindful Farewell to the Day

As the day winds down, create a mindful transition from work to leisure. Whether you're returning home from the office or wrapping up remote work, take a few moments to mentally close the door on the workday. Acknowledge your accomplishments, express gratitude for the day's experiences, and consciously shift your mindset from work mode to personal time. This mindful farewell to the day sets the stage for a more relaxed and rejuvenating evening.

Mindful Moments Before Bed

End your day with a few mindful moments that pave the way for restful sleep. As you prepare for bedtime, engage in a brief mindfulness practice. It could be a few minutes of deep breathing, a body scan to release tension, or a gratitude reflection where you mentally list a few things you're thankful for. Let go of the day's stresses and allow your mind to settle into a state of calm. As you drift off to sleep, you carry the serenity of mindfulness into your dreams.

Creating Mindful Anchors

Incorporating mindfulness into your daily routines isn't about adding extra tasks to your to-do list; it's about transforming existing moments into mindful anchors. These anchors serve as reminders to bring your attention back to the present, fostering a sense of grounding and peace throughout the day. Whether you're brushing your teeth, walking to a meeting, or waiting for your coffee to brew, these moments become opportunities to reconnect with the present.

Mindfulness is a Journey, Not a Destination

As you infuse mindfulness into your daily routines, remember that it's a journey, not a destination. There will be days when your mind is more scattered, and that's okay. The essence of mindfulness lies in the practice, in the intention to be present with whatever arises. It's a gentle, ongoing exploration that unfolds with each breath, step, and moment of awareness.

So, my fellow mindfulness explorers, let's embark on this journey of infusing daily routines with the magic of presence. As you sip your coffee, answer emails, or take a stroll, let mindfulness be your companion, turning the ordinary into the extraordinary. The adventure continues, and each mindful moment is a step toward a more intentional and fulfilling life. 🌟 🏞️

The Power of Gratitude Journaling

Greetings, gratitude enthusiasts! In this section, we're diving into the transformative world of gratitude journaling – a practice that turns ordinary moments into extraordinary sources of joy. Imagine it as a treasure hunt for the gems in your daily life, where every entry is a celebration of the simple, beautiful, and often overlooked blessings that surround you. So, grab your journal and a cup of tea, and let's explore the profound power of gratitude journaling, a practice that can infuse your days with positivity, mindfulness, and a deep sense of appreciation.

Unveiling the Magic of Gratitude

Gratitude journaling is like opening a window to let in the sunshine of positivity. It's about acknowledging and appreciating the good things, big or small, that enrich your life. The magic lies in the simplicity – no grand gestures or elaborate rituals required. With a pen and paper, or your favorite note-taking app, you're ready to embark on a journey of gratitude that can profoundly impact your outlook on life.

Starting Your Gratitude Journal

Begin by setting aside a few minutes each day to reflect on and jot down the things you're grateful for. It could be the warmth of sunlight streaming through your window, a kind word from a colleague, or the comforting aroma of your morning coffee. The key is to focus on specifics, allowing yourself to fully experience the richness of each moment.

The Ripple Effect of Gratitude

As you consistently engage in gratitude journaling, you'll begin to notice a ripple effect. The more you train your mind to seek out and appreciate the positive, the more positivity you attract. It's like planting seeds of gratitude that grow into a lush garden of joy. Studies have shown that regular gratitude practice is linked to increased well-being, improved mood, and a more optimistic outlook on life.

Gratitude for the Little Things

One of the beauties of gratitude journaling is its ability to magnify the significance of seemingly small moments. Whether it's the gentle rustle of leaves on a quiet afternoon, the taste of your favorite snack, or the feeling of fresh, crisp sheets against your skin, these details become treasures when seen through the lens of gratitude. The practice encourages you to savor the richness of your daily experiences.

The Gratitude Ripple in Relationships

Gratitude has the remarkable power to strengthen connections with others. Consider incorporating expressions of gratitude for people in your life into your journal. It could be a heartfelt note of appreciation to a friend, a thank-you text to a family member, or simply jotting down a moment that made you grateful for a colleague. As you share your gratitude, you not only uplift others but also deepen your own sense of connection and belonging.

Navigating Challenges with Gratitude

Gratitude isn't just reserved for the smooth sailing moments of life; it can be a compass that guides you through challenging waters. When facing difficulties, use your gratitude journal to anchor yourself in the positive aspects of your situation. Perhaps there's a lesson to be learned, a silver lining to be found, or even a moment of support or kindness that emerged amidst the challenges. Gratitude becomes a tool for resilience, helping you navigate adversity with a mindset of strength and growth.

Making Gratitude a Daily Habit

For gratitude journaling to weave its magic, consistency is key. Make it a daily habit, incorporating it into your routine at a time that feels natural for you. Whether it's in the morning to set a positive tone for the day or in the evening to reflect on the moments that brought you joy, find a rhythm that works best. The more you make gratitude a regular part of your day, the more it becomes second nature, transforming your mindset over time.

Creativity in Gratitude Journaling

Feel free to get creative with your gratitude journaling. It's your personal space to express gratitude in a way that resonates with you. Consider adding doodles, quotes, or even photos that capture the essence of your moments of appreciation. The goal is to make your gratitude journal a delightful and personal reflection of the positivity in your life.

Gratitude Challenges and Themes

To keep your gratitude practice fresh and engaging, consider incorporating challenges or themes into your journaling. Challenge yourself to find three new things to be grateful for each day, or dedicate a week to expressing gratitude for specific aspects of your life, such as relationships, work, or personal achievements. Themes add a playful element to your practice and deepen your exploration of gratitude.

Reflection and Celebration

Periodically, take a moment to review your gratitude journal. It's a journey map of your positive experiences and a testament to the richness of your life. Celebrate the patterns you observe, the personal growth you've experienced, and the ever-expanding circle of gratitude in your life. Your gratitude journal is not just a record; it's a celebration of the beauty that surrounds you.

The Gratitude Ripple in Self-Care

Gratitude and self-care go hand in hand. As you cultivate gratitude, you become more attuned to your own well-being. Use your gratitude journal to express thanks for the ways you've taken care of yourself – whether it's a moment of rest, a healthy meal you enjoyed, or a decision that prioritized your happiness.

Gratitude becomes a mirror reflecting the self-care practices that contribute to your overall well-being.

The Journey Continues: Gratitude as a Way of Life

Incorporating gratitude journaling into your routine isn't just a practice; it's a way of life. It's about cultivating a mindset that embraces the positive, even in the midst of life's challenges. As you continue this journey, remember that gratitude isn't limited to extraordinary moments; it's a celebration of the everyday magic that surrounds you. Your gratitude journal is your compass, guiding you toward a life illuminated by the radiant light of appreciation. The adventure continues, and each expression of gratitude is a step toward a more joyful and fulfilled existence.
🌈✨

Chapter 4: Outdoor and Nature-Based Self-Care

Hello, fellow nature enthusiasts! Chapter 4 invites you to step into the rejuvenating embrace of the great outdoors, where the symphony of rustling leaves, the dance of sunlight through the trees, and the crisp breeze become your companions on the journey to well-being. Consider this chapter your passport to the natural wonders that surround us, a guide to unlocking the transformative power of outdoor and nature-based self-care. Whether you're a seasoned adventurer or someone who prefers a leisurely stroll, we're about to explore the myriad ways nature can become your sanctuary, offering solace, joy, and a deep connection to the world around you. So, lace up your walking shoes, grab your water bottle, and let's embark on an exploration of the incredible benefits that await when you open the door and step outside into the embrace of Mother Nature. Get ready to breathe in the fresh air, bask in the sunlight, and discover the magic that unfolds when you make the great outdoors your personal playground of well-being! 🍃🌞

The Therapeutic Benefits of Nature

Welcome to the green wonderland, where the trees whisper secrets, the breeze carries serenity, and every step feels like a dance with tranquility. In this section, we're unraveling the therapeutic tapestry of nature, exploring the profound impact the great outdoors has on your well-being. It's not just about scenic views and Instagram-worthy landscapes; it's about the therapeutic embrace of nature that can rejuvenate your mind, body, and soul.

The Nature Prescription: Stress Reduction

Consider nature your doctor's prescription for stress reduction, and the best part? No copays required. Stepping into nature triggers a physiological response that reduces the production of stress hormones. The gentle rustle of leaves, the rhythmic lapping of water, or the chorus of birdsong can create a natural symphony that calms the nervous system. So, when life gets a bit too hectic, consider a nature break your antidote to stress.

The Mood-Boosting Magic of Green Spaces

Feeling a bit blue? Nature's got your back. Research suggests that spending time in green spaces is linked to improved mood and reduced feelings of anxiety and depression. Whether it's a sprawling park, a wooded trail, or even a community garden, the vibrant green hues act like a mood-boosting paintbrush, infusing your spirit with a sense of vitality and positivity. So, the next time you need a pick-me-up, head outdoors and let the colors of nature paint your mood brighter.

Mindfulness in Motion: Nature Walks and Meditation

Nature is the ultimate mindfulness guru, offering a plethora of opportunities for being fully present. A leisurely stroll through a nature reserve or a seated meditation session under a tree can become immersive experiences of mindfulness. The sights, sounds, and scents of nature anchor your attention to the present moment, creating a mental sanctuary where worries take a backseat, and the beauty of now takes center stage.

Sunshine Vitamin: Nature's Vitamin D Boost

Nature doesn't just nurture your mind; it's a supplier of the sunshine vitamin – vitamin D. Exposure to sunlight triggers the synthesis of vitamin D in your skin, a crucial nutrient for bone health, immune function, and overall well-being. So, while you're out there basking in the natural glow, your body is soaking up not just the beauty around you but also a dose of vitamin D, nature's own health elixir.

Healing Sounds of Nature: Birdsong and Beyond

Ever found solace in the sound of waves crashing on the shore or the gentle hum of a forest breeze? Nature's symphony goes beyond the visual feast, encompassing a rich auditory experience. Birdsong, running water, wind through the leaves – these sounds have a therapeutic quality, reducing stress and promoting a sense of calm. Consider it a playlist composed by Mother Nature herself, customized for your well-being.

Grounding: Earthing for Physical and Mental Balance

Take off your shoes and feel the earth beneath your feet – that's the essence of grounding, or earthing.

Connecting with the ground, whether it's soil, grass, or sand, is believed to have numerous health benefits. It's like plugging into the Earth's energy source, promoting physical balance and mental clarity. So, kick off those shoes and let the earth's grounding embrace recalibrate your energy.

Biophilia: The Innate Connection with Nature

Ever wondered why a walk in the woods or a day at the beach feels like a return to your true self? It's called biophilia – the innate connection between humans and nature. We're hardwired to seek out and thrive in natural environments. From the savannahs where our ancestors roamed to the urban parks where we find respite today, nature is woven into the fabric of our well-being. Embracing this connection is like coming home to a place where your soul feels nourished and understood.

Nature's Reset Button: Cognitive Restoration

Feel your brain's energy reserves running low? Nature is the ultimate reset button for cognitive restoration. Research indicates that spending time in nature enhances attention and focus while reducing mental fatigue. So, when the demands of daily life have your brain doing acrobatics, consider a nature break your secret weapon for mental rejuvenation.

Social Nature: Connection and Community

Nature isn't just a solitary retreat; it's also a hub for connection and community. Whether it's a group hike, a picnic in the park, or a community garden project, nature provides a backdrop for social bonding. The shared experience of nature fosters a sense of belonging and camaraderie, reminding us that our well-being is intertwined with the well-being of others.

Creating Your Nature Rituals

Incorporating nature into your self-care routine doesn't require a grand expedition. It can be as simple as a daily stroll in a nearby park, a weekend hike, or even a moment of stillness in your backyard. The key is to make nature a consistent part of your routine, allowing its therapeutic benefits to weave seamlessly into your life. So, whether you're a seasoned outdoor enthusiast or a newbie to nature's wonders, consider this your invitation to embrace the healing embrace of the great outdoors. The adventure continues, and the trails of well-being await – let's explore them together! 🌳🌼

Budget-Friendly Outdoor Activities

Calling all thrifty adventurers! In this section, we're diving into the treasure trove of budget-friendly outdoor activities, proving that a journey into nature doesn't have to break the bank. Whether you're a penny-pincher, a frugal friend, or simply looking for wallet-friendly ways to embrace the great outdoors, we've got you covered. Let's explore a variety of activities that allow you to bask in the beauty of nature without sending your budget into a tailspin.

Picnics in the Park: A Feast for the Senses

Gather your favorite snacks, pack a blanket, and head to the nearest park for a picnic extravaganza. Picnics offer a delightful blend of nature, good food, and relaxation. Whether you're solo, with a friend, or rounding up the whole crew, a picnic is a budget-friendly way to enjoy the outdoors. Bonus tip: Opt for reusable containers and utensils to keep it eco-friendly.

Trail Blazing on a Budget: Hiking Adventures

Hiking is the classic budget-friendly outdoor activity, offering a myriad of trails for all skill levels. Lace up your sneakers, grab a water bottle, and hit the trails for a nature-infused workout. Many hiking trails are free or have a minimal entrance fee, making it an accessible option for nature lovers on a budget. Pack a homemade trail mix, and you've got the perfect snack for your budget-friendly adventure.

Botanical Garden Bliss: Floral Escapes

Botanical gardens are like nature's art galleries, showcasing a stunning array of flowers, plants, and landscapes. Many botanical gardens offer free or discounted admission on certain days or during specific times. Take a leisurely stroll, breathe in the floral scents, and let the beauty of nature surround you without burning a hole in your wallet.

Nature Photography Safari: Capture the Moment

Transform your outdoor excursion into a photography safari. Grab your smartphone or a budget-friendly camera and set off to capture the beauty of nature. From the intricate details of leaves to panoramic landscapes, photography allows you to immerse yourself in the present moment while creating lasting memories. Share your snaps with friends or turn them into budget-friendly décor for your space.

Yoga in the Park: Zen on a Budget

Bring your yoga mat or a blanket, find a serene spot, and let the park become your yoga studio. Many parks offer open spaces perfect for a budget-friendly yoga session. Whether you're a seasoned yogi or a beginner, practicing yoga in nature adds an extra layer of tranquility to your routine. Check local community calendars for free or donation-based outdoor yoga events.

Geocaching Adventures: A Modern Treasure Hunt

Embark on a real-life treasure hunt with geocaching. All you need is a smartphone with a geocaching app, and you're ready to discover hidden treasures in outdoor locations. Geocaching is a global, community-driven activity that combines adventure, technology, and the thrill of discovery – all on a budget-friendly scale.

Stargazing Soiree: Cosmic Connections

Nature doesn't clock out when the sun sets. Turn your gaze skyward and indulge in the celestial wonders of stargazing. Find a spot away from city lights, lay out a blanket, and let the night sky be your budget-friendly canvas. You might even catch a meteor shower or spot constellations. Stargazing is a reminder that the universe's grandeur is the ultimate budget-friendly show.

Beach Day Bonanza: Sandy Serenity

If you're lucky enough to live near a beach, seize the opportunity for a budget-friendly beach day. Enjoy the sun, sand, and surf without spending a fortune. Pack your own snacks, sunscreen, and a good book for a relaxing day by the ocean. Pro tip: Check if your local beach has free entry or reduced rates during certain times.

Biking Bliss: Two-Wheeled Adventures

Cycling is not only a budget-friendly mode of transportation but also a fantastic way to explore outdoor spaces. Whether it's a leisurely ride along a scenic path or a more adventurous mountain biking trail, cycling allows you to cover more ground while embracing the beauty of nature. Dust off that bike and pedal your way to budget-friendly bliss.

Volunteer in the Great Outdoors: Give Back and Connect

Combine your love for nature with the spirit of giving by volunteering in outdoor conservation projects. Many organizations welcome volunteers for activities like trail maintenance, tree planting, and park cleanups. It's a budget-friendly way to make a positive impact on the environment while fostering a deeper connection with the great outdoors.

Remember, the beauty of budget-friendly outdoor activities lies not only in their affordability but in the joy, relaxation, and connection they bring. Nature is a generous host, offering a wealth of experiences that won't drain your wallet. So, whether you choose a picnic, a hike, or a photography safari, the great outdoors is your budget-friendly playground of well-being. The adventure continues, and the possibilities are as vast as the landscapes that await you. 🌳🌲

Cultivating a Connection with Nature for Mental Well-Being

Greetings, nature enthusiasts! In this section, we're delving into the art of cultivating a meaningful connection with the natural world for the betterment of your mental well-being. Nature is not just a backdrop; it's a therapeutic ally, a confidant, and a source of profound mental rejuvenation. So, let's embark on a journey to explore how fostering a genuine connection with nature can become a cornerstone of your mental wellness routine.

Mindful Nature Walks: A Symphony of Senses

Nature walks are more than just a stroll; they're an opportunity to engage all your senses. As you walk through a forest, a park, or along a beach, take a moment to truly observe. Feel the texture of leaves, listen to the rustle of branches, and breathe in the earthy aroma. Engaging your senses in this way transforms your walk into a mindful journey, grounding you in the present moment and allowing nature to become a canvas for mental well-being.

The Healing Power of Green Spaces

Surrounding yourself with greenery is like a tonic for the mind. Green spaces, whether it's a park, a garden, or a tree-lined street, have a calming effect on the nervous system. The color green is associated with tranquility and renewal, providing a visual respite from the hustle and bustle of daily life. So, seek out these pockets of green paradise to nurture your mental well-being.

Nature as a Stress-Buster: Unplug and Unwind

Modern life is a whirlwind of screens, notifications, and constant connectivity. Nature offers a welcome escape from this digital barrage. Consider your outdoor excursions a chance to unplug and unwind. Leave the phone in your pocket, resist the urge to check emails, and let the soothing sounds of nature replace the cacophony of notifications. It's a budget-friendly and effective stress-buster available to you whenever you step outside.

The Art of Sit Spot: Finding Stillness

Discover the magic of the sit spot – a designated place in nature where you simply sit and observe. It could be a quiet corner of your backyard, a park bench, or a cozy rock by the river. The goal is to find a spot where you can be still and present. As you sit, let your mind quieten, observe the natural world around you, and relish the sense of peace that comes from embracing stillness in nature.

Nature Journaling: Words Among the Wildflowers

Give your thoughts a home among the wildflowers by starting a nature journal. Record your observations, jot down your feelings, or even sketch the landscapes that captivate you. Nature journaling is a therapeutic outlet for self-expression, allowing you to document your connection with the natural world. It's a personal journey that intertwines your mental well-being with the beauty of the outdoors.

Sunshine Serotonin: Harnessing Natural Light

Sunlight isn't just a mood enhancer; it's a serotonin booster. Serotonin, often referred to as the "feel-good" neurotransmitter, increases with exposure to natural light. So, when you soak up the sun during your outdoor adventures, you're not just getting a dose of vitamin D; you're also tapping into nature's serotonin-rich source, lifting your spirits and fostering mental well-being.

Forest Bathing: Immersing in Nature's Healing Aura

Originating from Japan, shinrin-yoku, or forest bathing, is a practice that involves immersing yourself in the atmosphere of the forest. It's not about hiking or exercise; it's about absorbing the healing energy of the trees. As you stroll through the forest, let go of distractions, breathe deeply, and allow the therapeutic aura of the trees to envelop you. Forest bathing is a sensory experience that invites tranquility and mental rejuvenation.

Connecting with Wildlife: Nature's Companions

Whether it's observing birds in your backyard, watching fish swim in a pond, or encountering wildlife on a hike, connecting with the animal kingdom is a powerful way to foster a sense of connection with nature. Animals move with a natural rhythm, reminding us to slow down, be present, and appreciate the simple joys of observation. Consider it a delightful reminder that you're not alone in the great outdoors.

Earthing for Mental Clarity: Barefoot Connection

Kick off your shoes and experience earthing – direct physical contact with the earth. Whether it's walking barefoot on grass or feeling the coolness of soil beneath your feet, earthing is believed to promote mental clarity and reduce stress. It's a simple yet profound way to enhance your connection with nature and ground yourself in the present moment.

Creating Rituals of Connection: Consistency is Key

Cultivating a connection with nature is not a one-time endeavor; it's a relationship that thrives on consistency. Establish rituals that anchor your connection, whether it's a weekly nature walk, a monthly sit spot session, or a daily moment of gratitude for the natural world. Consistency deepens your bond with nature and allows its mental well-being benefits to become an integral part of your life.

As you cultivate a genuine connection with nature, remember that it's a dynamic relationship that evolves with each encounter. Nature becomes a partner in your mental well-being journey, offering solace, inspiration, and a profound sense of connection. So, my fellow nature enthusiasts, embrace the therapeutic embrace of the outdoors, let the mental well-being adventure continue, and may your connection with nature be as deep as the roots of the ancient trees that stand witness to the beauty that surrounds us. 🪶🌲

Chapter 5: Nourishing Your Body on a Budget

Hello, budget-conscious foodies! Chapter 5 invites you to embark on a culinary adventure where wholesome nutrition meets wallet-friendly choices. In the realm of self-care, nourishing your body is a cornerstone, and the good news is you don't need a hefty grocery bill to achieve it. This chapter is your guide to navigating the aisles, filling your cart with nutritious goodies, and creating budget-friendly, palate-pleasing meals that celebrate the joy of eating well without breaking the bank. From savvy shopping tips to delicious, budget-friendly recipes, we're about to unlock the secrets of nourishing your body on a budget. So, grab your shopping list and a sprinkle of culinary enthusiasm – let's explore how to make every meal a feast of well-being that your body and your wallet will thank you for. Get ready to savor the flavors of budget-friendly nourishment as we dive into the delectable world of chapter 5! 🍎 🥦

Budget-Friendly Meal Planning

Hey savvy chefs! In this section, we're diving into the delightful world of budget-friendly meal planning – a game-changer for both your well-being and your wallet. Meal planning is like giving your kitchen a superhero cape; it saves time, minimizes food waste, and ensures your taste buds are in for a treat without draining your budget. So, put on your apron, grab a pen, and let's explore the art of crafting delicious, nutritious meals without breaking the bank.

Master the Art of Batch Cooking: Cooking in Batches, Savoring in Portions

Batch cooking is your secret weapon in the battle against budget strain. Dedicate a day to whip up large quantities of versatile ingredients like grains, proteins, and veggies. Divide them into portions and freeze for later use. This not only saves time during hectic weekdays but also prevents you from resorting to pricey takeout when you're short on time. From hearty stews to flavorful grains, batch cooking opens the door to a variety of budget-friendly meal possibilities.

Embrace Versatile Ingredients: The Budget Maestros

Certain ingredients are budget maestros – they're versatile, affordable, and can transform into a variety of dishes. Think rice, beans, lentils, and pasta. These pantry staples can be the foundation for countless budget-friendly meals. Get creative with spices, sauces, and herbs to add flair and flavor without breaking the bank. Versatility is the key to keeping your taste buds entertained while sticking to your budget.

Shop Smart: The Budgeter's Guide to Grocery Shopping

Navigating the grocery store like a budget pro involves a strategic approach. First, create a shopping list based on your planned meals for the week. Stick to the list to avoid impulse purchases. Opt for generic brands, explore bulk bins for cost-effective staples, and be on the lookout for sales and discounts. Buying in-season fruits and veggies not only saves money but also ensures freshness and flavor. With a little strategic shopping, you'll leave the store with bags full of budget-friendly goodness.

Flexible Meal Prep: Tailoring to Your Schedule

Meal prep doesn't have to be an elaborate Sunday affair. Embrace a flexible approach that aligns with your schedule. It could mean preparing components of meals in advance, like chopping veggies or marinating proteins. Flexibility allows you to integrate meal prep seamlessly into your routine, making it a sustainable practice rather than a daunting task. The goal is to make nourishing choices convenient and budget-friendly.

Repurpose Leftovers: The Remix Masters

Leftovers are not just a replay of yesterday's meal; they're an opportunity for culinary creativity. Transform last night's roasted veggies into a vibrant stir-fry or repurpose that cooked chicken into a flavorful wrap. The art of remixing leftovers not only prevents food waste but also adds excitement to your weekly menu without requiring additional grocery expenses. It's like giving your taste buds a surprise party with familiar ingredients in a new ensemble.

DIY Convenience Foods: Budget-Friendly and Customizable

Say goodbye to expensive pre-packaged convenience foods and hello to the DIY version. Whether it's granola bars, salad dressings, or spice blends, making these items at home not only saves money but also allows you to customize flavors to your liking. Invest in basic staples, and you'll have the foundation for creating a variety of budget-friendly, homemade convenience foods that align with your well-being goals.

Explore Frozen and Canned Options: The Budget-Friendly Lifesavers

Frozen fruits, veggies, and canned goods are budget-friendly lifesavers that retain their nutritional value. They have a longer shelf life, reducing the risk of food waste. Keep your freezer stocked with frozen veggies for quick stir-fries, and canned beans for protein-packed salads. These budget-friendly options are not only convenient but also versatile, adding a nutritional boost to your meals without a hefty price tag.

Plan for Flexibility: Budget-Friendly Culinary Adventures

While planning is key, leave room for culinary adventures. Be open to trying new recipes, experimenting with different ingredients, and embracing the occasional indulgence. Flexibility in your meal plan allows you to adapt to unexpected schedule changes or take advantage of last-minute sales. It's the perfect balance between structure and spontaneity, making budget-friendly meal planning a sustainable and enjoyable practice.

Community Resources: Budget-Friendly Collaborations

Explore community resources that offer budget-friendly options. Farmers' markets, community-supported agriculture (CSA), and local food co-ops often provide fresh, affordable produce. Consider joining a community garden for access to fresh vegetables or connect with neighbors for ingredient-sharing initiatives. Community collaboration not only enhances your budget-friendly meal options but also fosters a sense of connection and shared well-being.

Celebrate Small Victories: Budget-Friendly Feasts

Nourishing your body on a budget is a series of small victories. Celebrate each successful meal prep, each budget-friendly grocery haul, and each delicious, wallet-friendly creation. By acknowledging your achievements, you reinforce the positive impact of budget-friendly meal planning on your well-being and financial goals. Every budget-friendly feast is a step toward a healthier, happier you.

As you dive into the world of budget-friendly meal planning, remember that it's not just about saving money; it's about savoring the joy of nourishing your body with wholesome, delicious choices. The adventure continues, and your kitchen is the canvas for a masterpiece of well-being that won't break the bank. So, my fellow budget-conscious chefs, let's turn every meal into a celebration of affordability, flavor, and the joy of eating well on a budget! 🍴🍽️

Nutrient-Dense Foods That Won't Break the Bank

Hello, budget-conscious health enthusiasts! In this section, we're diving into the world of nutrient-dense foods that not only enrich your well-being but also keep your wallet happy. Who said eating nutritiously has to come with a hefty price tag? Let's explore a variety of budget-friendly, nutrient-packed options that will make your taste buds dance without sending your budget into a frenzy.

Eggs: The Protein Powerhouses

Eggs are the unsung heroes of budget-friendly nutrition. Packed with high-quality protein, essential vitamins, and minerals, eggs are a versatile ingredient that can be the star of any meal. Whether scrambled for breakfast, hard-boiled for a snack, or added to fried rice for dinner, eggs are a nutrient-dense, budget-friendly option that won't crack your budget.

Beans and Legumes: Plant-Powered Protein

Beans and legumes are the champions of plant-powered protein and budget-friendly nutrition. Whether it's black beans, lentils, or chickpeas, these humble legumes are rich in fiber, protein, and a host of essential nutrients. They're the foundation for hearty soups, stews, and salads that fill you up without emptying your wallet. Embrace the versatility of beans to create budget-friendly, nutrient-dense meals.

Oats: The Fiber-Fueled Breakfast Staple

Oats are the fiber-fueled breakfast staple that keeps both your digestive system and your budget on track. Whether in the form of oatmeal, granola, or overnight oats, this budget-friendly grain provides a sustained energy boost and a wealth of essential nutrients. Customize your oats with budget-friendly toppings like fruits, nuts, and seeds for a nutrient-dense morning delight.

Canned Fish: Omega-3 Rich Bargains

Don't overlook the budget-friendly treasures in the canned fish aisle. Tuna, salmon, and sardines are omega-3 rich options that offer a burst of heart-healthy benefits without breaking the bank. Canned fish can be tossed into salads, sandwiches, or pasta dishes, providing a convenient and nutrient-dense addition to your budget-friendly repertoire.

Frozen Fruits and Vegetables: Nature's Budget Bounty

Enter the frozen aisle for a budget-friendly bounty of fruits and vegetables. Frozen produce retains its nutritional value and often comes at a lower cost than fresh counterparts. Whether you're blending frozen berries into a smoothie, tossing frozen veggies into a stir-fry, or using them as a side dish, frozen fruits and vegetables are nutrient-dense options that bring color and vitality to your plate without compromising your budget.

Sweet Potatoes: Budget-Friendly Beta-Carotene

Sweet potatoes are not just a vibrant addition to your plate; they're a budget-friendly source of beta-carotene, a precursor to vitamin A. Packed with fiber and various vitamins and minerals, sweet potatoes can be baked, mashed, or roasted for a nutrient-dense side dish or the star of a budget-friendly main course.

Whole Grains: Budget-Friendly Fiber Boosters

Whole grains like brown rice, quinoa, and barley are budget-friendly fiber boosters that elevate your meals' nutritional profile. These grains provide sustained energy, aid in digestion, and offer a range of essential nutrients. Incorporate whole grains into your budget-friendly meal planning for a satisfying and nutrient-dense foundation.

Greek Yogurt: Protein-Packed Elegance

Greek yogurt is the elegant, protein-packed guest at your budget-friendly feast. Rich in protein, probiotics, and calcium, Greek yogurt adds a creamy and nutritious touch to both sweet and savory dishes. Create budget-friendly parfaits with Greek yogurt, fruits, and granola or use it as a creamy base for sauces and dressings that enhance your nutrient-dense culinary creations.

Cabbage: The Budget-Friendly Cruciferous King

Cabbage, the unsung hero of the produce section, is a budget-friendly cruciferous king that boasts a myriad of health benefits. Packed with vitamins, minerals, and antioxidants, cabbage is a versatile vegetable that can be shredded for slaws, sautéed as a side dish, or fermented into budget-friendly sauerkraut for gut health. This budget-friendly gem proves that nutrient density doesn't have to come with a hefty price tag.

Peanut Butter: Budget-Friendly Nutrient Bliss

Peanut butter, the classic spread that transcends generations, is a budget-friendly nutrient bliss. Packed with healthy fats, protein, and essential nutrients, peanut butter is a versatile ingredient that adds flavor and nutrition to your budget-friendly meals. Spread it on whole grain toast, swirl it into oatmeal, or use it as a base for budget-friendly sauces and dressings.

Navigating the aisles with a focus on nutrient-dense, budget-friendly options opens up a world of culinary possibilities that support both your well-being and your financial goals. These budget-friendly superstars prove that nourishing your body doesn't have to be a luxury; it can be a daily celebration of delicious, nutrient-packed choices. So, my fellow budget-conscious nutrition enthusiasts, let's continue our journey into the world of affordable and nutrient-dense delights! 🥜 🧄

Affordable Ways to Stay Hydrated and Energized

Hey, budget-friendly hydrators and energizers! In this section, we're unlocking the secrets to keeping your body fueled and energized without burning through your budget. Staying hydrated and maintaining energy levels are essential components of well-being, and the good news is that you don't need a bottomless wallet to achieve it. Let's explore a variety of affordable and delightful ways to quench your thirst and boost your energy levels without breaking the bank.

Water: The Ultimate Budget-Friendly Elixir

Let's start with the OG of hydration – water. It's the ultimate budget-friendly elixir that not only keeps you hydrated but also supports overall health. Invest in a reusable water bottle and carry it with you throughout the day. Not only does this practice save money on single-use bottles, but it also serves as a constant reminder to sip and stay energized. Jazz up your water with a splash of lemon or cucumber for a refreshing twist.

Homemade Infusions: Flavorful and Budget-Friendly

Elevate your hydration game with homemade infusions. Grab your favorite fruits, herbs, and even a few slices of cucumber or a handful of berries. Toss them into a pitcher of water and let the natural flavors infuse. This budget-friendly alternative to store-bought flavored water not only keeps things interesting but also encourages you to reach your hydration goals without sacrificing your budget.

Budget-Friendly Herbal Teas: Sip and Thrive

Herbal teas are budget-friendly hydrators with added health benefits. Explore an array of flavors like peppermint, chamomile, or ginger. Purchase in bulk to save even more. Herbal teas are not only soothing but also contribute to your daily fluid intake. Sip on a warm cup during chilly evenings or enjoy it over ice for a refreshing twist – a budget-friendly journey to hydration heaven.

DIY Electrolyte Drinks: Hydration on a Budget

Rehydrate like a pro with DIY electrolyte drinks. Instead of splurging on commercial sports drinks, create your own by mixing water with a pinch of salt, a splash of citrus juice, and a touch of honey for sweetness. This budget-friendly concoction replenishes electrolytes without the added sugars and costs. It's a simple and effective way to stay energized without draining your wallet.

Coconut Water: Nature's Hydration Boost

If you're looking for a natural hydration boost, consider coconut water. It's a budget-friendly alternative to sports drinks, providing electrolytes without artificial additives. Look for sales and purchase in larger quantities to maximize your budget-friendly hydration. Coconut water is not only refreshing but also adds a tropical twist to your hydration routine.

Budget-Friendly Smoothies: Blend and Thrive

Smoothies are a versatile and budget-friendly way to stay hydrated while boosting your energy levels. Use affordable, nutrient-dense ingredients like frozen fruits, yogurt, and a handful of leafy greens. Experiment with different combinations to find your perfect budget-friendly blend. Smoothies are not only delicious but also provide a convenient option for staying nourished and hydrated on a budget.

Chia Seeds: Hydration Warriors

Chia seeds are tiny hydration warriors that pack a nutritional punch. When soaked in water, chia seeds form a gel-like consistency that helps retain hydration. Add a spoonful to your water, yogurt, or smoothies for a budget-friendly boost of omega-3 fatty acids and fiber. Chia seeds are an affordable and versatile addition to your hydration arsenal.

Citrus Fruits: Budget-Friendly Vitamin C

Citrus fruits, like oranges and grapefruits, are not only rich in vitamin C but also excellent sources of hydration. Purchase in-season citrus fruits to take advantage of lower prices and enhanced flavor. Slice them up for a refreshing snack or infuse your water with citrusy goodness. These budget-friendly fruits add a zing of flavor and nutrition to your hydration routine.

Green Tea: Antioxidant Elixir on a Budget

Green tea is a budget-friendly antioxidant elixir that contributes to both hydration and energy levels. Purchase in bulk to maximize savings, and enjoy it hot or cold. Green tea contains a modest amount of caffeine, providing a gentle energy boost without the jitters. Sip on this budget-friendly elixir for a delightful and healthful hydration experience.

Homemade Energy Bites: Budget-Friendly Fuel

For a budget-friendly energy boost, whip up some homemade energy bites. Combine ingredients like oats, nut butter, honey, and a sprinkle of seeds. These nutrient-dense bites are not only a tasty snack but also provide a sustainable source of energy. Make a batch at the beginning of the week and enjoy a budget-friendly pick-me-up whenever you need an energy boost.

Staying hydrated and energized on a budget is not only achievable but also a delightful journey into the world of creative and affordable hydration options. These budget-friendly strategies not only support your well-being but also prove that nourishing your body doesn't have to come with a hefty price tag. So, my fellow budget-conscious hydrators and energizers, let's raise a glass to affordable well-being and the joy of staying hydrated and energized on a budget! 🥤💪

Chapter 6:
Exercise and Movement on a Budget

Hello, budget-friendly fitness enthusiasts! Chapter 6 invites you to lace up your sneakers, grab your workout mat, and join the movement without putting a strain on your wallet. Embracing a physically active lifestyle doesn't have to break the bank, and in this chapter, we're going to explore a variety of affordable and enjoyable ways to get your body moving. Whether you're a fitness novice or a seasoned enthusiast, we've got budget-friendly tips, tricks, and strategies to make exercise a joyful and accessible part of your well-being routine. From DIY home workouts to creative outdoor activities, let's dive into the world of movement on a budget, where every step, stretch, and jump brings you closer to a healthier, happier you. Get ready to discover the joy of staying active without sweating over your finances – because a budget-friendly approach to fitness is not just good for your body; it's great for your wallet too! 🏋️ 💡 🏃 🤸

Exploring Low-Cost or Free Fitness Options

This section is your passport to a world of exercise and movement that won't make a dent in your wallet. We're diving into the realm of low-cost or free fitness options, proving that you don't need a fancy gym membership or pricey equipment to break a sweat and stay active. Let's explore a variety of budget-friendly avenues that will have you moving, grooving, and embracing the joy of fitness without the financial stress.

YouTube Workouts: The Virtual Gym at Your Fingertips

Say hello to your virtual gym! YouTube is a treasure trove of free workout videos, catering to every fitness level and preference. From high-intensity interval training (HIIT) to yoga and dance workouts, the options are endless. Fitness influencers and certified trainers offer step-by-step guidance, turning your living room into a bustling workout studio. It's a budget-friendly fitness adventure with the added benefit of flexibility – choose workouts that suit your schedule and fitness goals without spending a dime.

Fitness Apps: Personal Trainer in Your Pocket

Turn your smartphone into a personal trainer with budget-friendly fitness apps. Many apps offer free workout routines, ranging from beginner to advanced levels. Whether you're into running, bodyweight exercises, or guided yoga sessions, these apps provide structured workouts without costing you a penny. It's like having a fitness expert in your pocket, guiding you through exercises and tracking your progress without breaking your budget.

Community Classes: Gathering for Fitness

Explore local community classes that offer budget-friendly or donation-based fitness sessions. Many communities organize group workouts in parks, community centers, or even online. Joining these classes not only keeps you active but also allows you to connect with like-minded individuals. Whether it's a weekend yoga session in the park or a group run through your neighborhood, community classes are a fantastic way to stay fit on a budget while fostering a sense of belonging.

Outdoor Activities: Nature's Gym

Nature has its own gym, and the best part is, it's free! Take advantage of outdoor activities like hiking, jogging, cycling, or even a simple walk in the park. Mother Nature provides the perfect backdrop for your workout, offering fresh air, scenic views, and the added bonus of vitamin D from sunlight. Outdoor activities not only contribute to your physical well-being but also provide a mental health boost, making it a budget-friendly and holistic approach to staying active.

Library Resources: Fitness for the Mind and Body

Your local library is not just a haven for books; it's a resource for budget-friendly fitness too. Many libraries offer workout DVDs that you can borrow for free. From classic aerobics to pilates and dance workouts, you can find a variety of exercise routines to suit your preferences. It's a cost-effective way to diversify your fitness routine without spending money on specialized workout programs.

DIY Home Gym: Budget-Friendly Equipment Alternatives

Creating a home gym doesn't have to drain your bank account. Get creative with budget-friendly alternatives to traditional exercise equipment. Use household items like water bottles as weights, a sturdy chair for step-ups, or a towel for resistance exercises. You can even repurpose a backpack as a weighted vest. DIY home gyms allow you to stay active without investing in expensive equipment, proving that a budget-friendly approach to fitness is all about ingenuity.

Local Parks and Recreation Programs: Budget-Friendly Fitness Events

Check out your local parks and recreation programs for budget-friendly fitness events. Many cities organize free fitness classes, from boot camps to group runs, in public spaces. These events often feature local instructors or trainers, creating a sense of community while keeping your fitness expenses in check. Whether it's a weekend Zumba class in the park or a group cycling event, local programs provide accessible and enjoyable ways to stay active on a budget.

Online Challenges and Communities: Budget-Friendly Accountability

Joining online fitness challenges and communities adds a social and accountable dimension to your budget-friendly fitness journey. Many platforms and social media groups organize challenges that encourage participants to complete specific workouts or achieve fitness goals. The communal aspect provides support, motivation, and a sense of accountability without costing you a dime. It's a virtual fitness buddy system that makes staying active on a budget a fun and collaborative experience.

University or College Resources: Student-Accessible Fitness

If you're a student, tap into university or college resources for budget-friendly fitness options. Many educational institutions offer free or heavily discounted fitness classes, access to sports facilities, or intramural sports programs. Take advantage of these student-accessible resources to stay active without straining your budget. It's a fantastic way to prioritize your well-being while making the most of the amenities provided by your academic institution.

Public Trails and Paths: Explore the Great Outdoors

Discover public trails and paths in your area for a budget-friendly outdoor workout. Whether it's a walking trail, a jogging path, or a cycling route, public outdoor spaces provide a scenic and cost-free environment for exercise. Lace up your sneakers, grab your bike, or simply take a brisk walk – exploring the great outdoors is a budget-friendly fitness adventure that brings the added benefit of connecting with nature.

Embarking on a budget-friendly fitness journey is not just about saving money; it's about making movement and well-being accessible to everyone. These low-cost or free fitness options prove that staying active can be joyful, diverse, and budget-friendly. So, my fellow budget-conscious fitness enthusiasts, let's lace up those sneakers, hit play on that workout video, and embrace the joy of moving without the financial strain! 🏋️ ♂ 🚴 ♀

Creating a Budget-Friendly Home Workout Space

Hey budget-friendly fitness champions! In this section, we're transforming a corner of your home into a budget-friendly workout haven. Who says you need a high-end gym membership or fancy equipment to break a sweat? Let's explore creative and affordable ways to carve out a home workout space that suits your lifestyle, enhances your well-being, and doesn't break the bank.

Choose the Right Space: Where Comfort Meets Motivation

Look around your home for a space that resonates with you. It could be a corner of the living room, a spot in the bedroom, or even a cozy corner of the balcony. The key is to find a space that feels comfortable and inspires motivation. Consider natural light, good ventilation, and enough room for movement. Your budget-friendly workout space should be a sanctuary that makes you excited to move.

Declutter and Rearrange: Free Up Your Fitness Zone

Before you bring in any equipment, declutter the chosen space. Remove unnecessary items and create an open, inviting atmosphere. Rearrange furniture if needed to maximize the available space. A clutter-free environment not only makes your workout space visually appealing but also allows for unrestricted movement. It's a budget-friendly way to transform your space without spending a dime.

DIY Yoga and Exercise Mat: Comfort Without the Cost

Investing in a high-quality mat doesn't have to be a budget buster. Create your own DIY yoga or exercise mat by repurposing items you already have. An old towel or blanket folded neatly can serve as a cushioned surface for floor exercises. Not only does this save money, but it also adds a personal touch to your budget-friendly workout space. It's comfort without the cost!

Resistance Bands: Budget-Friendly Strength Training

Enter the world of resistance bands – the budget-friendly superheroes of strength training. These versatile bands provide resistance for various exercises and take up minimal space. They're affordable, portable, and perfect for toning muscles without splurging on hefty weights. Incorporate resistance bands into your budget-friendly home workout space for a cost-effective strength training experience.

DIY Weights: Household Items Turned Fitness Equipment

Say goodbye to expensive dumbbells and hello to DIY weights made from household items. Fill up water bottles, grab a sturdy backpack and load it with books, or use canned goods as makeshift weights. These budget-friendly alternatives offer resistance for a variety of exercises without requiring a dedicated budget for fitness equipment. It's a creative and affordable way to add strength training to your home workout space.

Jump Rope: Budget-Friendly Cardio Blast

Jump ropes are not just for the schoolyard; they're budget-friendly cardio tools that elevate your heart rate without emptying your wallet. An affordable jump rope provides an effective cardiovascular workout, improves coordination, and adds a fun element to your home workout space. It's a cost-effective way to infuse your routine with bursts of high-intensity cardio.

Incorporate Stability: Budget-Friendly Balance Boosters

Enhance your home workout space by incorporating stability elements. A stability ball, often available at an affordable price, adds an element of core engagement to your exercises. Use it for sit-ups, planks, or even as a chair for seated exercises. Stability cushions or discs are additional budget-friendly options that improve balance and strengthen stabilizing muscles. These low-cost additions turn your home workout space into a dynamic and engaging fitness zone.

Utilize Bodyweight Exercises: No Equipment, No Problem

Don't underestimate the power of bodyweight exercises – they're the foundation of budget-friendly fitness. Squats, lunges, push-ups, and planks require no equipment, making them perfect for your home workout space. Use your body as resistance and leverage different variations to target various muscle groups. It's a cost-free and efficient way to build strength, flexibility, and endurance in your budget-friendly fitness sanctuary.

DIY Mirror: Reflecting Success on a Budget

Create a DIY workout mirror to visually expand your home workout space and check your form. Repurpose an old mirror or purchase an affordable one and mount it strategically in your workout area. A mirror not only adds a touch of elegance but also serves as a valuable tool for maintaining proper posture and ensuring you're getting the most out of each exercise. It's a budget-friendly way to reflect on your fitness journey.

Personalized Motivation: Budget-Friendly Inspirational Decor

Infuse your budget-friendly workout space with personalized motivation. Print out motivational quotes, frame them, and hang them on the wall. Use affordable decals or create your own artwork to inspire positivity and perseverance. Your home workout space is not just a physical environment; it's a mental sanctuary for motivation and well-being. Adding personalized touches is a budget-friendly way to create a space that reflects your fitness journey.

Creating a budget-friendly home workout space is all about ingenuity, resourcefulness, and a sprinkle of creativity. Transforming your living space into a fitness haven doesn't require a hefty budget; it's about maximizing what you have and adding budget-friendly elements that enhance your exercise experience. So, my fellow budget-conscious fitness enthusiasts, let's roll out those yoga mats, grab our DIY weights, and revel in the joy of movement without the financial strain! 🏋️💪

Incorporating Movement into Your Daily Routine Without Spending Money

Hey there, budget-savvy movers and shakers! In this section, we're breaking down the misconception that staying active requires a hefty price tag. Let's explore creative and cost-free ways to infuse movement into your daily routine, proving that you don't need a gym membership or pricey equipment to keep your body in motion. Get ready to discover the joy of incorporating movement into your day without spending a dime!

Take the Stairs: A Vertical Adventure

Turn the mundane act of climbing stairs into a vertical adventure! Whether at home, work, or out in public spaces, opt for stairs instead of elevators or escalators. It's a simple yet effective way to engage your leg muscles, boost your heart rate, and burn a few extra calories—all without spending a penny. Embrace the ascent and descent as a budget-friendly mini-workout that adds movement to your daily routine.

Walking Meetings: Stride and Strategize

Trade the conference room for a walking path during meetings. Walking meetings not only add steps to your daily count but also stimulate creativity and productivity. Whether you're discussing projects with colleagues or catching up with friends, the act of moving enhances the conversation. It's a budget-friendly way to incorporate movement into your workday without the need for special equipment or financial commitment.

Dance Breaks: Groove Your Way to Fitness

Who says you need a dance studio or a dance fitness class? Crank up your favorite tunes and turn your living room into a dance floor. Dance breaks are a fun and cost-free way to elevate your heart rate, improve coordination, and, most importantly, have a good time. Whether you're a seasoned dancer or just moving to the beat, dancing is a joyful and budget-friendly way to incorporate movement into your day.

Desk Exercises: Stretch, Strengthen, and Sit

Don't let a desk job hinder your movement goals. Incorporate simple exercises at your desk to stretch and strengthen your muscles. Try seated leg lifts, desk push-ups, or neck stretches. These desk exercises not only break up periods of sitting but also contribute to better posture and reduced muscle stiffness. It's a budget-friendly solution for staying active during office hours without spending a dime on fancy equipment.

Parkour Playfulness: Urban Movement Adventure

Channel your inner ninja with a bit of parkour playfulness. Urban environments offer various surfaces and structures that can become your budget-friendly playground. Jump over low obstacles, balance on curbs, or perform controlled landings. Parkour is a creative and freeform way to engage your entire body in movement. Just be sure to choose safe environments and start with beginner-friendly moves to avoid injuries.

Bodyweight Exercises: Sculpting Without Spending

Your body is a versatile piece of equipment. Leverage bodyweight exercises to sculpt and tone your muscles without spending a dime. Squats, lunges, planks, and push-ups are excellent examples of bodyweight exercises that engage multiple muscle groups. Create a routine that suits your fitness level and goals. It's a budget-friendly way to build strength and endurance using the most accessible tool—your own body.

Outdoor Adventures: Nature's Fitness Playground

Explore the great outdoors for a budget-friendly fitness adventure. Hiking, biking, jogging, or even a simple nature walk—all these activities allow you to engage with the natural environment and get your body moving. Parks, trails, and open spaces offer a plethora of opportunities for outdoor movement without the need for pricey memberships. Nature's fitness playground is vast, and it's yours to explore without spending money.

Gardening Workout: Cultivate Fitness

Turn your gardening sessions into a workout routine. Digging, planting, weeding, and watering involve various muscle groups and provide a low-impact form of exercise. Gardening not only beautifies your outdoor space but also contributes to your daily movement goals. It's a budget-friendly way to blend the benefits of physical activity with the joys of cultivating a green space.

Active Commuting: Move While You Move

Transform your daily commute into an active adventure. If possible, consider walking or biking to work. Not only does this save money on transportation, but it also adds valuable movement to your day. If your commute involves public transportation, consider getting off a stop earlier and walking the remaining distance. Active commuting is a budget-friendly way to incorporate movement into your routine while reducing your carbon footprint.

Playful Recreation: Games for Fitness

Rediscover the joy of playful recreation. Engage in activities like frisbee, basketball, or even a game of tag with friends or family. These games not only offer a budget-friendly way to stay active but also add an element of fun and social interaction. It's a reminder that movement doesn't have to be a chore; it can be a delightful and cost-free part of your daily routine.

Incorporating movement into your daily routine without spending money is all about embracing creativity, spontaneity, and the innate joy of being active. These simple yet effective strategies prove that staying fit doesn't require an expensive gym membership or high-end equipment. So, my fellow budget-savvy movers, let's step, sway, and dance our way to a healthier, happier, and more active lifestyle—without spending a penny! 🏃‍♂️🕺

Chapter 7:
Emotional Well-Being on a Shoestring Budget

Hello, budget-friendly souls seeking a dose of emotional well-being! Chapter 7 is your guide to nurturing your mental and emotional health without breaking the bank. In a world that often feels fast-paced and financially demanding, it's essential to prioritize our emotional well-being. This chapter is a treasure trove of affordable strategies, actionable tips, and heartfelt advice to help you navigate the ups and downs of life without a hefty price tag. From simple self-care practices to embracing gratitude on a budget, we're delving into the art of cultivating emotional well-being with creativity, compassion, and a dash of frugality. Get ready to discover how small, budget-friendly actions can lead to significant emotional dividends, making your journey toward mental wellness both accessible and delightful. Because when it comes to emotional well-being, the best things in life truly are free or, at the very least, budget-friendly! 🎇 📶

Affordable Therapy Options

Hey there, budget-conscious champions of emotional well-being! In this section, we're diving into the world of affordable therapy options, because taking care of your mental health shouldn't come with a hefty price tag. Whether you're navigating life's challenges, seeking personal growth, or just in need of someone to talk to, there are budget-friendly avenues to explore. Let's unpack some creative and accessible ways to prioritize your mental and emotional well-being without burning through your wallet.

Community Mental Health Clinics: Accessible Support

Community mental health clinics are hidden gems in the world of affordable therapy. Many communities offer low-cost or sliding-scale fee services, making professional mental health support accessible. These clinics are staffed by licensed therapists and counselors who provide a range of services, from individual therapy to group sessions. Check with local health departments or non-profit organizations to discover community mental health resources that align with your budget.

Therapist Directories: Connecting with Affordability*

Explore therapist directories that specialize in affordable options. Online platforms like Open Path Collective connect individuals with mental health professionals who offer services at reduced rates. These directories are a valuable resource for finding licensed therapists who are committed to making mental health support affordable. It's a budget-friendly way to connect with professionals who understand the importance of accessible mental health care.

University Counseling Centers: Student-Priced Wisdom

If you're a student, tap into university counseling centers for budget-friendly therapy options. Many educational institutions offer counseling services to students at reduced rates or even for free. These services are often provided by graduate students under the supervision of licensed professionals. It's an excellent opportunity to access quality mental health support without straining your budget, all while contributing to the learning experience of future mental health professionals.

Teletherapy Platforms: Digital Support on a Budget

Embrace the convenience and affordability of teletherapy platforms. Online counseling services, such as BetterHelp and Talkspace, connect users with licensed therapists through virtual sessions. Many of these platforms offer more budget-friendly rates compared to traditional in-person therapy. The flexibility of scheduling and the comfort of receiving support from your own space make teletherapy a practical and affordable choice for prioritizing your emotional well-being.

Non-Profit Organizations: Compassion Meets Affordability

Non-profit organizations dedicated to mental health often provide affordable or free counseling services. These organizations prioritize accessibility and work with qualified professionals who are committed to giving back to the community. Reach out to mental health non-profits in your area to inquire about available services. Many of them offer support groups, counseling, and educational resources at little to no cost.

Employee Assistance Programs (EAP): Workplace Well-Being

Check if your workplace offers an Employee Assistance Program (EAP). EAPs typically provide employees with access to counseling services, often at no cost or a minimal fee. These programs recognize the importance of supporting employees' mental health and well-being. If your workplace has an EAP, take advantage of this budget-friendly resource to address personal or work-related challenges with the guidance of a professional.

Support Groups: Shared Wisdom, Shared Costs

Consider joining support groups focused on specific challenges or themes. Many support groups, whether in-person or online, operate on a peer support model, offering a sense of community and understanding. While not a replacement for professional therapy, support groups can be a valuable complement to your mental health journey. Some groups may operate on a donation basis, making it a budget-friendly option for connecting with others who share similar experiences.

Books and Self-Help Resources: Budget-Friendly Insights

Don't underestimate the power of self-help resources. Books, workbooks, and online resources cover a wide range of mental health topics. While they don't replace the personalized guidance of a therapist, these resources can provide valuable insights, coping strategies, and exercises to support your emotional well-being. Visit your local library or explore online platforms for budget-friendly self-help materials.

Sliding Scale Services: Tailoring Costs to Your Budget

Many private practitioners offer sliding scale services, adjusting their fees based on your financial situation. If you find a therapist you resonate with, don't hesitate to inquire about sliding scale options. Therapists understand that financial constraints shouldn't be a barrier to mental health support and may be willing to work with you to find a fee that aligns with your budget.

Mental Health Apps: Pocket-Friendly Wellness

Explore budget-friendly mental health apps that offer guided exercises, mindfulness practices, and mood tracking. While these apps don't replace therapy, they can be valuable tools for daily emotional well-being. Many apps offer free versions or have affordable subscription options, making them accessible to individuals on a budget.

Prioritizing your emotional well-being doesn't have to come with a hefty price tag. These affordable therapy options demonstrate that support, understanding, and guidance can be accessible to everyone, regardless of their financial situation. So, my budget-friendly warriors of emotional well-being, let's break down the barriers to mental health care and embark on a journey of self-discovery and resilience without breaking the bank! 🌈💜

Building a Support Network Without Financial Strain

Hey budget-savvy champions of emotional well-being! In this section, we're diving into the wonderful world of building a support network without breaking the bank. Because when it comes to navigating life's twists and turns, having a support system is like having a cozy blanket for your soul – and the best part is, you don't need a fortune to create one. Let's explore creative, heartfelt ways to surround yourself with support, understanding, and a network of caring individuals, all without a hefty financial burden.

Friendship Potlucks: Nourishing Connections, Budget Style

Invite friends over for a friendship potluck, where everyone brings a dish to share. Sharing a meal is a timeless way to bond, and a potluck ensures that the financial responsibility is distributed among the group. It's a budget-friendly way to create a warm, inviting space for connection and conversation without anyone feeling the strain on their wallets. Plus, who can resist the charm of a potluck where each dish tells a story?

Weekly Walk-and-Talks: Budget-Friendly Therapy

Turn your catch-ups into movement with weekly walk-and-talk sessions. Instead of meeting at a cafe, opt for a stroll in the park or around your neighborhood. Walking together not only provides the benefits of physical activity but also creates a relaxed environment for open conversations. It's a budget-friendly alternative to traditional meetups that fosters a sense of well-being for both body and mind.

Book Club Bliss: Budget-Friendly Learning and Connection

Start a budget-friendly book club with friends or join an existing one. Reading and discussing books not only offer intellectual stimulation but also provide an avenue for sharing thoughts and experiences. Many libraries offer book club kits with multiple copies of the same book, making it easy and cost-effective to get started. A book club is a fantastic way to build a support network while indulging your love for literature.

Skill Swap Sundays: Barter Your Way to Connection

Initiate a skill swap among your friends or within your community. Identify skills or talents each person possesses and offer to share them with others. Whether it's cooking, knitting, playing an instrument, or a knack for organizing, skill swap Sundays create a reciprocal environment where everyone contributes and benefits. It's a budget-friendly way to build connections based on shared interests and talents.

Community Events: Local Connections, No Cost

Explore free community events in your area, from festivals to workshops to volunteer opportunities. These events not only offer the chance to meet new people but also provide a sense of belonging to a larger community. Attend local gatherings, join community clean-up efforts, or participate in cultural events to build connections without spending money. It's a budget-friendly way to immerse yourself in the richness of your community.

Virtual Hangouts: Connecting Beyond Borders

Embrace the world of virtual hangouts to connect with friends and family, no matter the distance. Platforms like Zoom, Skype, or FaceTime allow you to host virtual gatherings, game nights, or simply catch up with loved ones. The beauty of virtual hangouts is their accessibility – no travel expenses, no need for elaborate setups. It's a budget-friendly way to stay connected, even if oceans or time zones separate you.

DIY Support Circles: Creating Your Safe Space

Form a DIY support circle with friends who share similar goals or challenges. Whether it's focused on personal development, health and wellness, or career aspirations, a support circle provides a safe space for open discussions and mutual encouragement. It's a budget-friendly way to build a close-knit support network that grows together, sharing triumphs and overcoming challenges collectively.

Social Media Support: Affirmation in the Digital Age

Harness the positive side of social media to build a support network. Join online communities or groups that align with your interests, passions, or challenges. These digital spaces can offer a sense of connection, shared experiences, and support without any financial investment. Engage in conversations, share your journey, and be open to the connections that can blossom in the virtual realm.

Gratitude Exchange: Budget-Friendly Positivity

Initiate a gratitude exchange with friends or family members. Regularly share what you're grateful for and encourage others to do the same. This simple practice fosters a positive and supportive atmosphere within your network. Gratitude exchanges can happen through text messages, emails, or even a dedicated group chat. It's a budget-friendly way to infuse your relationships with a spirit of appreciation and encouragement.

Outdoor Adventure Crew: Nature's Therapy, for Free

Connect with like-minded individuals who appreciate the outdoors. Whether it's hiking, camping, or simply exploring nature together, forming an outdoor adventure crew can be a budget-friendly way to build connections. Nature provides a therapeutic backdrop, and outdoor activities often require minimal or no financial investment. It's a delightful and refreshing approach to fostering connections while immersing yourself in the beauty of the great outdoors.

Building a support network without financial strain is all about creativity, shared experiences, and the genuine connections that enrich our lives. These budget-friendly ideas demonstrate that the most meaningful connections often come from simple, heartfelt gestures rather than extravagant spending. So, my budget-savvy champions of emotional well-being, let's weave a tapestry of support that nurtures, uplifts, and stands the test of time – all without putting a dent in our wallets! 🌸 🤍

Emotional Self-Care Practices That Require Minimal or No Spending

Hello, fellow advocates of emotional well-being on a budget! In this section, we're exploring the delightful realm of emotional self-care practices that won't make a dent in your wallet. Because, let's face it, taking care of your emotional health doesn't need to come with a hefty price tag. Get ready to discover a treasure trove of affordable and accessible practices that nourish your soul without draining your bank account.

Mindful Breathing: A Pocket-Sized Calm

One of the simplest and most effective emotional self-care practices is mindful breathing. Take a few moments each day to focus on your breath. Inhale deeply, hold for a moment, and exhale slowly. This practice requires no equipment, no apps, and no cost – just you and your breath. It's a pocket-sized calm that you can carry with you throughout the day, providing instant relief during moments of stress or overwhelm.

Gratitude Journaling: A Priceless Perspective Shift

Embrace the transformative power of gratitude journaling. Take a few minutes each day to jot down things you're grateful for. It could be a beautiful sunrise, a kind gesture, or simply the air you breathe. This practice requires nothing more than a notebook and a pen, making it an incredibly budget-friendly way to shift your perspective and cultivate a mindset of gratitude.

Daily Affirmations: Free Words of Encouragement

Create a list of daily affirmations to boost your confidence and self-esteem. Repeat these positive statements to yourself each morning or whenever you need a pick-me-up. Affirmations cost nothing but have the potential to create a positive impact on your emotional well-being. It's like giving yourself a daily dose of encouragement without spending a penny.

Nature Connection: Free Serenity

Immerse yourself in the therapeutic embrace of nature. Spend time outdoors, whether it's a walk in the park, sitting by a river, or simply enjoying the beauty of your backyard. Nature connection is a powerful emotional self-care practice that requires no financial investment. The calming effect of natural surroundings can bring serenity to your soul without costing a dime.

DIY Spa Day: Luxurious Self-Care at Home

Transform your home into a sanctuary of relaxation with a DIY spa day. Use items you already have, like candles, essential oils, and soothing music, to create a spa-like atmosphere. Pamper yourself with a warm bath, a face mask, or a simple hand massage. This budget-friendly indulgence is a treat for your senses and a nourishing practice for your emotional well-being.

Mindful Walking: Moving Meditation for Free

Turn your daily walks into mindful excursions. Pay attention to each step, the sensation of your feet on the ground, and the rhythm of your breath. Mindful walking is a form of moving meditation that requires no special equipment or financial investment. It's a simple yet powerful way to center yourself, reduce stress, and enhance your emotional well-being.

Digital Detox: Priceless Mental Clarity

Give yourself the gift of a digital detox. Set aside dedicated time each day to disconnect from screens and immerse yourself in analog activities. Read a physical book, go for a technology-free walk, or engage in a hobby that doesn't involve screens. This practice is not only budget-friendly but also offers priceless mental clarity and a break from the digital noise that can impact your emotional state.

Creativity Corner: Express Yourself Without Cost

Tap into your creative side as a form of emotional expression. Whether it's drawing, writing, singing, or any other artistic endeavor, use creativity as a tool for self-care. This practice requires minimal or no spending, as you can work with basic art supplies or use what you already have at home. Expressing your emotions through creativity is a therapeutic and budget-friendly way to nurture your emotional well-being.

Laughter Therapy: The Ultimate Free Medicine

Engage in laughter therapy without spending a dime. Watch a funny movie, listen to a comedy podcast, or spend time with people who make you laugh. Laughter is a natural mood booster that costs nothing but has immeasurable benefits for your emotional well-being. It's a budget-friendly prescription for joy and lightness.

Silent Reflection: Budget-Friendly Inner Connection

Create moments of silent reflection in your day. Find a quiet space, close your eyes, and simply be present with your thoughts. This practice requires no financial investment and offers an opportunity for inner connection and self-awareness. It's a budget-friendly way to check in with yourself emotionally and cultivate a sense of inner calm.

Embracing emotional self-care doesn't have to strain your budget. These practices show that nurturing your emotional well-being can be simple, accessible, and, most importantly, affordable. So, my fellow budget-friendly advocates of emotional well-being, let's weave these practices into our daily lives and experience the profound impact they can have on our overall happiness and resilience! 🫰💟

Chapter 8:
Mindful Spending for Long-Term Well-Being

Greetings, mindful spenders and seekers of long-term well-being! Chapter 8 is your passport to financial harmony and lasting happiness. In a world often dominated by impulsive purchases and fleeting trends, we're embarking on a journey of mindful spending, where every dollar invested is a step toward a richer, more fulfilling life. Join me as we explore the art of intentional consumption, discovering how aligning our spending habits with our values can lead to not just financial stability, but a profound sense of well-being that transcends the momentary thrill of a purchase. Get ready to unlock the secrets of mindful spending, cultivate a healthy relationship with your finances, and build a future that reflects your true priorities. It's time to reimagine the way we approach money, one mindful purchase at a time, on a path to a more fulfilling and sustainable way of living. 🎇 🪭

Prioritizing Needs vs. Wants

Hey savvy spenders, welcome to the compass of mindful spending! In this section, we're diving into the age-old dilemma: needs versus wants. Navigating your financial ship through the seas of endless choices can be tricky, but fear not, we're here to unravel the secrets of distinguishing between the must-haves and the nice-to-haves. Picture this as your spending compass, guiding you toward a future where your financial decisions align with your true priorities. Let's set sail!

Needs: The Anchors of Financial Stability

Needs are the sturdy anchors that keep your financial ship stable. These are the essentials for a comfortable and secure life—food, shelter, clothing, healthcare, and the bills that keep the lights on. Identifying your needs is like mapping out the foundation of a sturdy financial house. Take a moment to list your non-negotiables, the things that contribute directly to your well-being and the stability of your household. Once you've anchored your needs, you gain a clear view of what truly matters in your financial journey.

Wants: The Adventurous Sail of Desires

Now, let's set sail into the ocean of wants. Wants are the adventurous sails that propel your financial ship beyond the basics. These are the desires, the wishes, the indulgences that add flavor to life. While wants are not inherently bad, it's crucial to differentiate them from needs. The latest gadget, trendy fashion piece, or dining at fancy restaurants—

all wonderful sails, but not necessary for the basic functioning of your financial ship. By identifying wants, you gain insight into your personal desires and preferences, allowing you to navigate the sea of choices with intention.

The Balancing Act: Harmony in Decision-Making

The art of mindful spending lies in the delicate balancing act between needs and wants. It's not about eliminating wants entirely but rather finding harmony in their integration. Consider needs as the sturdy base of your financial pyramid, providing stability and security. Wants, on the other hand, become the layers that add uniqueness and enjoyment to your financial journey. The key is to ensure that your financial ship remains upright and steady, not tilting dangerously toward excessive wants that may compromise your long-term well-being.

Budgeting Brilliance: Allocating Wisely

A budget is your trusty map in the world of mindful spending. Allocate your financial resources wisely by earmarking a substantial portion for needs and allocating a reasonable, intentional amount for wants. This budgeting brilliance ensures that you prioritize the essentials while leaving room for enjoyable experiences. Regularly review and adjust your budget as your circumstances change, allowing you to navigate the ever-shifting currents of life with flexibility and control.

Delayed Gratification: The Anchor of Future Well-Being

Practice the art of delayed gratification, the anchor that secures your financial ship for the long haul. While the allure of instant satisfaction is strong, consciously delaying certain wants can lead to greater rewards down the line. This doesn't mean depriving yourself but rather strategically planning and saving for those desires. Delayed gratification empowers you to invest in experiences and items that truly align with your values and contribute to your long-term well-being.

Reflect and Reframe: Shifting Perspectives

Periodically reflect on your spending habits and reframe your perspective. Ask yourself: Are my purchases aligned with my values and long-term goals? This self-awareness helps you make mindful decisions, preventing impulsive spending on fleeting wants. The power of reflection lies in its ability to illuminate the true impact of your financial choices, guiding you toward a path where each expenditure contributes to your overall well-being.

In the journey of mindful spending, distinguishing between needs and wants is the compass that keeps you on course. Needs anchor you in financial stability, while wants become the sails that carry you toward a life of richness and fulfillment. It's about finding the balance that aligns with your values, ensuring that your financial ship sails smoothly through the vast sea of choices. So, my mindful spenders, let's set our compass right, prioritize wisely, and navigate toward a future where our financial choices reflect the true essence of a well-lived life! ⚓ 🧭

Making Informed Choices When Investing in Well-Being

Ahoy, fellow navigators of well-being! In this section, we're hoisting the sails of informed choices as we explore the seas of investing in our long-term happiness. Buckle up for a journey where every expenditure is a deliberate investment in your well-being, and where financial decisions are made with the wisdom of a seasoned captain. Ready to chart a course towards a future where every penny spent is a step towards lasting fulfillment? Let's set sail!

Well-Being as a Holistic Investment

Consider well-being as a holistic investment portfolio, where each element contributes to the overall wealth of your life. This includes physical health, mental well-being, personal growth, and meaningful connections. By viewing well-being as a diversified investment, you're empowered to allocate resources to areas that genuinely enrich your life. From nutritious food that fuels your body to activities that nurture your soul, every investment contributes to the prosperity of your well-being portfolio.

Prioritizing Preventative Investments

Think of well-being investments as preventative measures rather than reactionary solutions. Prioritize actions that promote long-term health and happiness, such as regular exercise, a balanced diet, and stress-reducing activities. These preventative investments act as a shield, protecting your well-being against the storms of life. While it may not provide immediate gratification, the long-term dividends are immeasurable.

Educated Spending: Knowledge is Currency

In the realm of well-being, knowledge is the most valuable currency. Equip yourself with information about nutrition, mental health practices, and lifestyle choices that align with your goals. Attend workshops, read reputable sources, and consult professionals to make informed decisions. Educated spending ensures that your investments are aligned with your well-being objectives, minimizing the risk of impulse purchases that may not contribute meaningfully to your long-term happiness.

Quality Over Quantity: The Gold Standard

When investing in well-being, prioritize quality over quantity. This applies to everything from the food you consume to the products you use. Opting for high-quality, nourishing options may require a higher initial investment, but the long-term benefits far outweigh the upfront costs. Investing in quality experiences, relationships, and self-care practices elevates your well-being portfolio to gold-standard status, ensuring lasting satisfaction and fulfillment.

Investing in Experiences: Memories as Wealth

Allocate a portion of your well-being budget to experiences rather than material possessions. Research indicates that experiences contribute more significantly to long-term happiness than the accumulation of things. Whether it's a weekend getaway, a concert, or a cooking class, investing in experiences creates lasting memories that appreciate in emotional value over time. These investments add depth and richness to your well-being portfolio.

Emotional Well-Being: The Heart of the Portfolio

Place a special emphasis on investments that nurture your emotional well-being, as it is the heart of your well-being portfolio. This includes activities that bring joy, moments of connection with loved ones, and practices that promote mindfulness and resilience.

Investing in emotional well-being pays dividends in enhanced overall life satisfaction and the ability to navigate challenges with grace.

Mindful Consumption: The Captain's Wisdom

Practice mindful consumption as the captain of your well-being ship. This involves being present and intentional in every spending decision. Before making a purchase, ask yourself: Does this align with my values? Will it contribute to my long-term happiness? Mindful consumption empowers you to make choices that resonate with your authentic self, steering your well-being ship towards a fulfilling and purpose-driven destination.

Regular Portfolio Reviews: Adapt and Thrive

Just as a financial portfolio requires regular reviews, so does your well-being investment strategy. Assess your spending habits, activities, and overall well-being regularly. Adapt your investment strategy based on changing circumstances and priorities. Regular portfolio reviews ensure that your well-being investments remain aligned with your evolving goals, allowing you to thrive in every chapter of your life.

In the voyage of mindful spending, making informed choices when investing in well-being is the compass that guides you towards a future rich in fulfillment and happiness. It's about recognizing the interconnectedness of your choices, understanding the value of preventative investments, and navigating the seas of well-being with wisdom and intention. So, my well-being investors, let's set our sails high, invest wisely, and chart a course toward a future where our well-being portfolio reflects the true wealth of a life well-lived! 🏦 🤍

Cultivating a Healthy Relationship with Money

Ahoy, financial navigators! In this section, we're embarking on the transformative journey of cultivating a healthy relationship with money. Picture this as tending to the soil of your financial garden, where the seeds you plant today bloom into a lush and bountiful future. Ready to discover the keys to a harmonious connection with your finances? Let's dig in and cultivate a relationship with money that blossoms into long-term well-being!

Understanding Money as a Tool, Not a Master

Money is a tool, a means to an end, not the master of your destiny. Cultivate a mindset that views money as a resource for achieving your goals and enhancing your well-being. Recognize that your worth extends far beyond your financial status. When money is seen as a tool, you gain the power to wield it consciously, directing it toward endeavors that align with your values and contribute to your long-term happiness.

Defining Financial Values: Anchors of Decision-Making

Anchor your relationship with money by defining your financial values. What matters most to you? Is it financial security, experiences, philanthropy, or a combination? Clarifying your financial values becomes the guiding light in decision-making. When faced with choices, refer back to your values to ensure that your financial ship stays on course, navigating the seas of spending with purpose and intention.

Budgeting as a Compass: Navigating with Precision

Consider budgeting as the compass that keeps you on track in your financial voyage. A budget is not a restriction; it's a tool that empowers you to allocate resources consciously. Create a budget that aligns with your financial values, allocating funds to needs, wants, and well-being investments. A well-crafted budget provides the precision needed to navigate the often unpredictable waters of financial decision-making.

Embracing Financial Literacy: Empowerment through Knowledge

Empower yourself by embracing financial literacy. Just as a gardener learns about soil, sunlight, and water, understanding financial principles gives you the knowledge needed to nurture your financial garden. Educate yourself on budgeting, investing, and managing debt. The more financially literate you become, the more confidently you can navigate the landscape of financial choices, sowing seeds of prosperity and avoiding potential pitfalls.

Mindful Spending: Consciously Tending to Your Garden

Practice mindful spending as the act of consciously tending to your financial garden. Before making a purchase, pause and reflect. Ask yourself: Does this align with my values? Is it a responsible use of my resources? Mindful spending ensures that each financial decision is intentional, contributing to the growth and well-being of your financial garden rather than fostering weeds of regret.

Gratitude for Abundance: Fertilizing Your Financial Soil

Cultivate gratitude for the abundance in your life. Just as a gardener appreciates the richness of the soil, acknowledge the financial blessings you have. Gratitude is the fertilizer that enriches your financial soil, allowing your resources to multiply and grow. When you approach your finances with a grateful heart, you create a positive and nurturing environment for your financial garden to flourish.

Addressing Money Mindset Weeds: Tackling Negative Beliefs

Identify and address the weeds in your money mindset—the negative beliefs or behaviors that hinder your financial growth. Whether it's fear of scarcity, avoidance of financial matters, or impulsive spending, tackling these weeds head-on is essential for a healthy relationship with money. Seek support, whether through financial counseling, self-help resources, or discussions with trusted friends. Clearing these weeds allows the true potential of your financial garden to shine.

Regular Financial Check-Ups: Pruning and Nurturing

Just as a gardener conducts regular check-ups on their plants, schedule regular financial check-ups. Review your budget, assess your financial goals, and adjust your strategies as needed. Prune away unnecessary expenses, nurture your financial goals, and celebrate the growth you've achieved. Regular financial check-ups ensure that your financial garden remains vibrant and aligned with your evolving priorities.

Cultivating a healthy relationship with money is akin to tending to a flourishing garden. It requires understanding money as a tool, defining your financial values, and approaching financial decisions with mindfulness and gratitude. By nurturing your financial garden, you sow the seeds of long-term well-being and create a landscape of abundance. So, my financial gardeners, let's cultivate a relationship with money that blossoms into a future rich in prosperity, purpose, and fulfillment! 🌱 💰

Chapter 9:
Community Resources and Support

Greetings, fellow travelers on the path to well-being! Chapter 9 beckons us into the heart of our journey, where the landscape transforms into a vibrant community of shared resources and support. In this chapter, we're diving into the wealth that community connections offer—resources, encouragement, and a sense of belonging that enhances our collective well-being. Imagine this as a communal potluck, where each brings something valuable to the table, creating a feast of support for everyone involved. Ready to explore the tapestry of community resources and discover how interconnectedness can elevate your well-being? Let's embark on a joyous exploration of the boundless treasures that community brings to our individual and collective flourishing! 💥 🤝

Identifying Local Resources for Affordable Self-Care

Hello, well-being enthusiasts! In this section, we're unraveling the hidden gems in our local communities—resources that often sparkle with affordability and accessibility. Your community is a treasure trove of support for your self-care journey, offering a tapestry of opportunities to nurture your well-being without breaking the bank. Let's embark on a quest to uncover these local gems and weave them into our self-care routine, creating a symphony of well-being that resonates from the heart of our neighborhoods.

Community Centers: Hubs of Well-Being

Start your exploration at the heart of your community—local community centers. These hubs often host a variety of affordable classes and activities, from yoga and meditation sessions to art workshops and fitness classes. Many community centers offer discounted or even free programs, making them accessible to all. Check out their schedule, and you might discover a new passion or a relaxing activity that fits perfectly into your self-care routine.

Public Parks: Nature's Self-Care Haven

Nature is an unparalleled source of well-being, and your local parks are nature's gift to your community. Take advantage of the green spaces for outdoor workouts, picnics, or simply unwinding in the fresh air. Some parks even host community events, providing opportunities for connection and shared well-being experiences. The best part? Enjoying the therapeutic benefits of nature is often entirely free!

Local Libraries: Wisdom at Your Fingertips

Your local library isn't just a haven for book lovers; it's a goldmine of resources for well-being enthusiasts. Many libraries host wellness programs, book clubs, and workshops on various self-care topics. Dive into their offerings, and you might find a wealth of knowledge, guidance, and a supportive community of fellow seekers.

Community Gardens: Cultivating Well-Being

If you have a green thumb or aspire to develop one, community gardens are the perfect place to nurture your well-being. These communal spaces not only offer the therapeutic benefits of gardening but also provide a sense of community and shared responsibility. Growing your own fruits, vegetables, or flowers can be a fulfilling and cost-effective way to enhance your well-being.

Local Meetup Groups: Shared Interests, Shared Well-Being

Explore online platforms like Meetup to find local groups centered around your interests. Whether it's a hiking club, a meditation circle, or a photography group, joining these gatherings connects you with like-minded individuals who share your passion for well-being. Many meetups are low-cost or free, offering a fantastic avenue for expanding your social circle while prioritizing self-care.

Fitness Classes in the Park: Nature-Fueled Exercise

Parks often host fitness classes, providing an outdoor alternative to pricey gym memberships. From yoga to boot camps, these classes leverage the natural surroundings for invigorating workouts. Check with your local parks and recreation department or fitness instructors who might offer classes at a nominal fee or even donation-based.

Volunteer Opportunities: Giving Back for Well-Being

Engaging in volunteer work not only benefits your community but also nourishes your well-being. Many organizations welcome volunteers, offering a chance to contribute to a cause you care about while fostering a sense of purpose and connection. The shared experience of giving back can be a powerful aspect of your self-care routine.

Local Farmers' Markets: Nutrient-Rich and Community-Rich

Farmers' markets are not just about fresh produce; they're vibrant community spaces. Explore your local market for affordable, locally sourced fruits, vegetables, and other goods. Connecting with local vendors and other shoppers enhances the sense of community, making your shopping experience a well-being boost.

Discounted Wellness Events: Well-Being on a Budget

Keep an eye out for discounted or free wellness events happening in your community. These could include health fairs, workshops, or wellness festivals. Local businesses and organizations often organize these events to promote well-being, providing an excellent opportunity to explore new practices and connect with professionals without a hefty price tag.

Senior Centers: Wise Wellsprings of Well-Being

Don't overlook the well-being wisdom found at local senior centers. Many offer affordable classes, social activities, and wellness programs that are open to all community members. Connecting with older individuals can bring a wealth of knowledge and experience to your well-being journey.

As you embark on the quest to identify local resources for affordable self-care, remember that your community is a rich tapestry of support waiting to enhance your well-being. Whether it's the tranquility of a community garden, the vitality of a local fitness class, or the wisdom found in a library workshop, these gems are woven into the fabric of your neighborhood, ready to elevate your self-care routine. So, my community explorers, let's embrace the wealth of well-being offerings in our local havens and create a symphony of self-care that resonates through our neighborhoods! 🏡🤝

Utilizing Community Programs and Services

Ahoy, well-being adventurers! In this section, we're setting sail to explore the bounty of community programs and services that await you. Your local community is not just a collection of places; it's a network of services designed to nurture the well-being of its residents. From health clinics to counseling services, community programs offer a diverse range of resources that can elevate your self-care journey. Let's navigate these seas of support and discover how tapping into community programs can enrich your well-being in ways both practical and profound.

Health Clinics and Screenings: A Checkup for Your Well-Being

Many communities host health clinics and screenings that provide essential services at little to no cost. From blood pressure checks to cholesterol screenings, these programs offer a proactive approach to your physical well-being. Keep an eye on local announcements for upcoming health events where you can access valuable information and services that contribute to a holistic approach to self-care.

Mental Health Services: Nurturing Your Emotional Well-Being

Your emotional well-being matters, and community programs often provide mental health services or counseling at reduced costs. Local clinics, non-profit organizations, or community centers may offer support groups, counseling sessions, or workshops. Don't hesitate to reach out and explore these services; taking care of your mental health is a crucial aspect of your overall well-being.

Community Education Programs: Wisdom for the Mind

Engage with community education programs that offer a wealth of knowledge on various well-being topics. These programs might cover nutrition, stress management, mindfulness, and more. Look out for workshops or seminars hosted by local experts, providing an opportunity to learn and grow in a supportive community setting.

Financial Wellness Workshops: Navigating the Seas of Finance

Communities often organize financial wellness workshops to empower residents with knowledge on budgeting, saving, and investing. Attend these sessions to gain valuable insights into managing your finances effectively, aligning your money habits with your well-being goals. Financial well-being is an integral part of the self-care journey, and these workshops can be a compass guiding you toward financial stability.

Job Assistance and Training Programs: Sailing Toward Career Well-Being

If career well-being is on your radar, explore job assistance and training programs offered by local organizations. These programs may provide career counseling, job search support, or skill-building workshops. Elevating your professional well-being can have a positive ripple effect on your overall sense of fulfillment and life satisfaction.

Family Support Services: Strengthening Your Support System

Communities often offer family support services, including parenting classes, support groups, and childcare resources. Strengthening your family support system contributes to your emotional well-being and provides a network of assistance when needed. These programs foster a sense of community and shared experiences among families.

Fitness and Wellness Classes: Energizing Your Body and Soul

Local community centers frequently host fitness and wellness classes that cater to various interests and fitness levels. From yoga and dance to meditation and group workouts, these classes offer a cost-effective way to prioritize physical well-being. Check out the schedules at community centers or inquire about classes organized by local fitness enthusiasts.

Nutrition Assistance Programs: Fueling Your Body Wisely

If maintaining a nutritious diet is a priority, explore nutrition assistance programs in your community. These may include food pantries, community gardens, or workshops on budget-friendly healthy eating. Accessing these resources ensures that you can nourish your body without straining your budget.

Community Engagement Initiatives: A Tapestry of Connection

Participate in community engagement initiatives that foster a sense of connection and belonging. These might include neighborhood clean-up events, community festivals, or volunteering opportunities. Engaging with your community on a broader level enhances your social well-being and strengthens the fabric of the community as a whole.

Transportation Services: Smoothing the Path to Well-Being

Accessing community programs and services is made easier with reliable transportation. Some communities offer transportation services for residents who may face mobility challenges. Explore these options to ensure you can effortlessly connect with the well-being resources available in your community.

As you set sail to utilize community programs and services, remember that your community is a wellspring of support waiting to elevate your self-care journey. Whether it's a health screening, financial workshop, or fitness class, these programs are designed to enhance your well-being in practical and meaningful ways. So, my well-being sailors, let's navigate the seas of community offerings, explore the riches available to us, and chart a course toward a future where our collective well-being flourishes! ⛵ 🌊

The Importance of Collective Well-Being

Ahoy, fellow champions of well-being! In this section, we're diving into the heart of the matter—the profound significance of collective well-being within our communities. As we navigate the seas of community resources and support, it becomes clear that our individual well-being is intricately woven into the fabric of the collective. Let's unravel the wisdom behind the idea that a rising tide lifts all boats and explore why fostering a sense of togetherness contributes not only to our personal flourishing but also to the vitality of the entire community.

The Ripple Effect of Well-Being

Picture a stone tossed into a serene pond—each ripple that emerges extends far beyond the point of impact. Similarly, our individual well-being creates a ripple effect within the community. When we prioritize self-care and engage with well-being resources, we contribute to a positive atmosphere that touches the lives of those around us. The smiles we share, the healthy habits we cultivate, and the support we offer create a tapestry of well-being that envelops the entire community.

Building Social Bonds: The Bedrock of Well-Being

Collective well-being is rooted in the bonds we build with our neighbors, friends, and fellow community members. Social connections are a fundamental aspect of well-being, providing a support system during challenging times and amplifying the joy during moments of celebration. Engaging in community programs fosters a sense of belonging, creating a network of relationships that enhances both individual and collective well-being.

Shared Resources, Shared Strength

Communities are like gardens where resources are the nutrients that nourish growth. By participating in and utilizing community programs, we contribute to the vitality of this shared garden. Whether it's accessing healthcare services, attending educational workshops, or benefiting from local initiatives, the utilization of these resources strengthens the community as a whole. As we share and support one another, the collective strength of the community grows, creating an environment where everyone can thrive.

Addressing Disparities: Bridging Gaps for All

A community's well-being is only as strong as its most vulnerable members. By recognizing and addressing disparities within our community, we contribute to a more equitable distribution of well-being. Accessible programs and services ensure that everyone, regardless of background or circumstances, has the opportunity to partake in the collective well-being journey. Bridging these gaps creates a more resilient and harmonious community.

Cultivating a Culture of Care

Individual well-being is intertwined with the culture of care that a community fosters. When we prioritize collective well-being, we cultivate a culture where acts of kindness, empathy, and support become the norm. Whether it's offering a helping hand to a neighbor, participating in community events, or volunteering time and skills, these actions collectively shape a culture of care that radiates positivity throughout the community.

Community Pride and Resilience

A community that prioritizes collective well-being fosters a sense of pride and resilience. When residents feel connected, supported, and proud of their community, they are more likely to invest time and effort into its well-being. This shared sense of pride becomes a source of resilience, empowering the community to face challenges with unity and determination.

Elevating the Local Economy

The well-being of a community is closely linked to its economic vibrancy. By participating in local programs and supporting community initiatives, we contribute to the economic health of the area. Local businesses thrive, job opportunities increase, and the overall prosperity of the community is uplifted. This economic well-being, in turn, supports the social and emotional fabric of the community.

A Legacy of Well-Being for Future Generations

Prioritizing collective well-being is an investment in the future. As we actively engage with community resources and support, we pave the way for future generations to inherit a legacy of well-being. The positive ripple effects of our actions echo through time, creating a foundation upon which future residents can build a flourishing community.

In the grand tapestry of well-being, the importance of collective well-being shines brightly. It's about recognizing that our individual journey is intertwined with the journeys of our neighbors, creating a harmonious symphony of well-being that resonates through the community. So, my well-being ambassadors, let's celebrate the interconnectedness of our lives, nurture the collective garden of well-being, and continue sailing toward a future where the entire community thrives! 🎇 🤝

Conclusion

Dear fellow self-care navigators, as we approach the final chapter of our well-being odyssey, it's time to reflect on the journey we've embarked upon together. In this concluding chapter, we stand at the summit, gazing back at the trails we've traversed—exploring the realms of self-care on a budget, uncovering the treasures within our communities, and embracing a holistic approach to well-being. Like a compass guiding us through uncharted waters, this book has been a companion on your quest for affordable and sustainable self-care. Now, as we gather our thoughts, let's celebrate the victories, acknowledge the challenges, and draw inspiration from the wisdom we've gathered. The conclusion is not just an end; it's a launchpad for the next phase of our self-care journey. So, my well-being pioneers, let's pen the final notes of this melody, knowing that the rhythm of self-care echoes through the chambers of our lives, sustaining us on the voyage ahead. 🧭 🌈

Key Takeaways

Ahoy, fellow travelers! As we gather around the well-being campfire to bid adieu to our self-care odyssey, let's reflect on the treasure trove of wisdom we've unearthed together. Our journey has been a kaleidoscope of discovery, weaving through the landscapes of budget-friendly self-care and community connection. Here, in the heart of our conclusion, let's distill the essence of our adventure into key takeaways that serve as lanterns guiding us forward.

Self-Care Beyond the Spa: Affordable and Attainable

In the opening chapters, we unraveled the myth that self-care is synonymous with expensive spa days and lavish retreats. Instead, we embraced a broader definition—one that celebrates everyday practices accessible to all. From mindful breathing to DIY spa days at home, we've learned that self-care is not a luxury; it's a fundamental right we can exercise with creativity and resourcefulness.

Navigating the Budget Seas: Financial Well-Being Matters

Our self-care voyage delved into the intricacies of budgeting, offering insights into creating a financial framework that supports well-being. We discovered that financial well-being isn't just about the numbers; it's a mindset that empowers us to make conscious choices aligned with our values. Setting realistic financial goals and cultivating a healthy relationship with money became our compass, ensuring our well-being journey stays on course.

Community: The Well-Being Anchor

Venturing into the heart of our communities, we uncovered a trove of resources and support. Community centers, local libraries, and even our neighborhood parks emerged as wellsprings of well-being. We learned that well-being isn't a solitary endeavor; it's a collective dance where each participant contributes to the rhythm of community connection. By identifying local resources and participating in community programs, we've strengthened the bonds that weave the fabric of well-being.

Affordable Practices, Profound Impact: Everyday Rituals

Chapter after chapter, we marveled at the potency of simple, everyday rituals in elevating our well-being. From mindful breathing exercises to cultivating gratitude through journaling, we discovered that the most impactful practices often reside in the realm of simplicity. These rituals, accessible to everyone, form the foundation of a resilient and sustainable self-care routine.

Nature's Embrace: Outdoor and Nature-Based Well-Being

Our journey took us outdoors, where we basked in the therapeutic embrace of nature. From budget-friendly outdoor activities to cultivating a connection with the natural world, we recognized that nature isn't just a backdrop; it's an active participant in our well-being journey. As we explored the therapeutic benefits of outdoor experiences, we discovered that the healing touch of nature is available to all, regardless of budget constraints.

Nourishing the Body: Affordable and Wholesome

In the realm of nourishment, we explored budget-friendly meal planning, nutrient-dense foods, and affordable ways to stay hydrated and energized. Breaking free from the notion that healthy eating is a privilege, we embraced the idea that well-balanced and nourishing meals can be accessible to everyone, enriching our bodies without burdening our wallets.

Movement as Medicine: Exercise on a Budget

The beats of our well-being melody resonated with the rhythm of movement. Exploring low-cost or free fitness options, creating a budget-friendly home workout space, and incorporating movement into daily routines, we discovered that exercise isn't confined to gym memberships or expensive equipment. Movement, as a form of self-care, is a celebration of what our bodies can achieve, accessible to all.

Emotional Well-Being: Nurturing the Heart

In the realm of emotional well-being, we navigated through affordable therapy options, building a support network without financial strain, and practicing emotional self-care that requires minimal or no spending. The conclusion is clear: emotional well-being is not a luxury; it's a vital aspect of our self-care journey that thrives on connection, support, and mindful practices.

Mindful Spending: A Path to Long-Term Well-Being

Our financial well-being expedition led us to the shores of mindful spending. We learned to distinguish between needs and wants, make informed choices when investing in well-being, and cultivate a healthy relationship with money. Mindful spending isn't about deprivation; it's about aligning our financial choices with our well-being goals, ensuring a sustainable and fulfilling future.

Community as a Well-Being Ecosystem: The Ripple Effect

In the final leg of our journey, we delved into the profound importance of collective well-being. We understood that our individual well-being is intricately connected to the well-being of our communities. Through shared resources, social bonds, and a culture of care, we contribute to a well-being ecosystem where the prosperity of one becomes the prosperity of all.

As we summarize these key takeaways, let's carry them forward as lanterns lighting the path to continued well-being. The chapters of this book are not just words on pages; they are waypoints in your ongoing journey—a journey where self-care, affordability, and community connection dance harmoniously. So, my well-being companions, let's embark on the next chapter of our adventure, armed with the wisdom we've gained, and continue sailing toward a future where our well-being flourishes like a garden in full bloom! 🏵️🏦

Empowering You to Prioritize Self-Care Within Your Financial Means

As we unfurl the sails for the final stretch of our self-care journey, let's navigate the waters of empowerment, anchoring the wisdom we've gathered into the fabric of your everyday life. This section isn't just a farewell; it's an invitation—a call to action that empowers you to prioritize self-care within the unique contours of your financial landscape. So, let's embark on this empowering voyage, charting a course toward well-being that aligns with your values, honors your financial means, and, most importantly, celebrates the resilient spirit of self-care.

Crafting Your Well-Being Blueprint

As you stand at the helm of your self-care journey, envision it as a canvas waiting for your strokes of well-being. Craft a well-being blueprint that aligns with your financial means, considering it not as a restriction but as a canvas that allows your creativity to flourish. Identify the self-care practices that resonate with you the most, integrating them into your daily life like brushstrokes creating a masterpiece.

The Power of Intention in Self-Care

Intention, dear travelers, is the wind in your sails. As you prioritize self-care within your financial means, infuse each practice with intention. Whether it's a mindful breathing exercise, a budget-friendly meal, or a nature-inspired outing, let intention be the guiding force. Your self-care journey is not a checklist; it's an intentional dance with well-being, where every step is a celebration of your commitment to yourself.

Redefining Luxury: Your Well-Being Oasis

Luxury isn't defined by the price tag; it's defined by the richness it brings to your life. In the realm of self-care, redefine luxury as moments that nourish your soul, irrespective of cost. Your well-being oasis might be a cozy corner with a good book, a simple yet delightful homemade meal, or a leisurely stroll in the park. By embracing the luxury of simplicity, you create a well-being sanctuary within your financial means.

Mindful Spending: Aligning Values with Choices

Mindful spending is the compass that ensures your financial ship sails in the direction of well-being. As you allocate funds for self-care, reflect on your values and priorities. Choose activities and practices that align with what truly matters to you. By making intentional and informed choices, you not only enhance your well-being but also cultivate a harmonious relationship with your finances.

Community Connections: The Currency of Well-Being

Community is a currency more valuable than gold on the well-being journey. Engage with your community, whether it's through local programs, shared resources, or simply fostering connections with neighbors. Community support is an enriching and often cost-effective aspect of self-care. Attend local events, join clubs, and participate in the vibrant tapestry of your community's well-being ecosystem.

Flexibility and Adaptability: Sailing Through Financial Storms

Life, much like the sea, is unpredictable. Financial storms may arise, and unforeseen circumstances may challenge your well-being voyage. In such times, remember the power of flexibility and adaptability. Self-care is not rigid; it's a resilient and adaptive practice. Be open to adjusting your sails, exploring new avenues, and finding solace in practices that bring well-being even during turbulent financial seas.

The Marathon of Self-Care: Sustainable Practices

Self-care is not a sprint; it's a marathon. As you prioritize well-being within your financial means, focus on sustainable practices that endure through time. Build habits that seamlessly integrate into your lifestyle, fostering a consistent and enduring well-being journey. Sustainable self-care is not about perfection; it's about progress, one step at a time.

Celebrating Progress: A Journey, Not a Destination

In this empowering chapter of our conclusion, let's celebrate progress over perfection. Your self-care journey is a continuous evolution, a dynamic dance with well-being that unfolds over time. Celebrate the small victories, the moments of joy, and the strides you make toward prioritizing self-care within your financial means. It's not about reaching a destination; it's about relishing the journey, cherishing the lessons, and reveling in the growth you experience along the way.

So, my empowered well-being navigators, as you set sail toward the horizon of self-care within your financial means, remember that this voyage is uniquely yours. Empowerment lies not in the grand gestures but in the daily choices that honor your well-being. May your journey be filled with the wind of intention, the compass of mindful spending, and the joy of community connections. Onward, towards a future where your well-being sails gracefully within the embrace of your financial means! ⚓ 🌊

Encouraging a Sustainable, Budget-Friendly Approach to Well-Being

Dear fellow well-being enthusiasts, as we near the final pages of our self-care saga, let's embrace the spirit of sustainability and forge a path forward that not only honors our financial means but also nurtures a lasting well-being legacy. In this concluding section, we're not just wrapping up; we're planting seeds of resilience, encouraging a sustainable, budget-friendly approach to well-being that will continue to bloom in the seasons to come.

The Tapestry of Sustainability

Picture your well-being journey as a vibrant tapestry woven with threads of intention, community, and mindful choices. Sustainability is the loom that holds this tapestry together, ensuring that it withstands the tests of time. As we encourage a sustainable approach to well-being, let's thread the needle of intentionality through the fabric of our lives, stitching together practices that endure beyond the ephemeral.

Holistic Well-Being: A Symphony of Practices

Sustainability in well-being is about harmony—a symphony of practices that resonate across physical, emotional, and social dimensions. Embrace practices that not only fit within your budget but also contribute to a holistic sense of well-being. From mindful breathing exercises to budget-friendly outdoor activities, let each note in your well-being symphony play a part in the harmonious orchestra of a balanced life.

Budget-Friendly Rituals: The Heartbeat of Daily Life

In the realm of well-being, rituals are the heartbeat of daily life. Cultivate budget-friendly rituals that anchor you in the present moment and infuse your days with purpose. Whether it's a morning stretch, an evening gratitude journaling session, or a weekly community engagement, these rituals become the steady rhythm that sustains your well-being journey, regardless of financial fluctuations.

Community Support: A Pillar of Resilience

Our well-being is not a solitary endeavor; it's a collaborative dance. Lean on the pillar of community support, nurturing connections that go beyond the transactional. Engage in the give-and-take of community life, recognizing that support, both emotional and practical, is a cornerstone of resilience. Together, we create a network that not only survives but thrives in the face of challenges.

DIY Well-Being: The Art of Resourcefulness

Resourcefulness is the secret sauce of sustainable well-being. Embrace the art of DIY well-being, where creativity and resourcefulness become your allies. From crafting budget-friendly home workout spaces to exploring DIY spa days, discover the joy that comes from creating well-being solutions with your own hands. The journey becomes not just about the destination but the process—the crafting of a well-being masterpiece.

Celebrating Affordability: Redefining Riches

Affordability isn't a limitation; it's a form of liberation. Celebrate the richness that budget-friendly well-being practices bring to your life. Redefine riches not in terms of monetary wealth but in the wealth of experiences, connections, and moments that contribute to your overall well-being. Your journey is a testament to the idea that true wealth lies in the richness of a well-lived life.

Hope as an Anchor: Navigating the Seas of Change

As we sail into the horizon of the last pages, let hope be our anchor. Change is the only constant, and life's seas may bring both calm and storms. Yet, with hope as our anchor, we navigate these waters with resilience and optimism. The sustainable, budget-friendly approach to well-being is not just a strategy; it's a mindset—a compass that guides us through the evolving landscapes of life.

A Hopeful Farewell: Continuity in Well-Being

As we bid farewell to these pages, let it be a hopeful adieu—a promise that your well-being journey continues, ever-evolving and flourishing. The bookends of our self-care exploration are not final; they are doorways to new beginnings. May your sails be filled with the winds of hope, your compass aligned with the values that matter, and your journey a tapestry woven with threads of joy, connection, and sustainable well-being.

So, my resilient companions, as you turn the last page and step into the horizon of your well-being future, do so with a heart full of hope and a spirit attuned to the melody of your own well-being song. The adventure doesn't end here; it transforms into the next chapter of your vibrant, sustainable, and budget-friendly well-being journey. Onward, towards a future where your well-being story unfolds with each step, a narrative of joy, resilience, and the enduring spirit of self-care. 🎋 ⚓ 🌈

9 798869 017345